STAND OUT

Evidence-Based Learning for College and Career Readiness

3

THIRD EDITION

STACI JOHNSON

ROB JENKINS

 NATIONAL GEOGRAPHIC LEARNING |  CENGAGE Learning

Australia • Brazil • Mexico • Singapore • United Kingdom • United States

Stand Out 3: Evidence-Based Learning for College and Career Readiness, Third Edition
Staci Johnson and Rob Jenkins

Publisher: Sherrise Roehr

Executive Editor: Sarah Kenney

Development Editor: Lewis Thompson

Director of Global Marketing: Ian Martin

Executive Marketing Manager: Ben Rivera

Product Marketing Manager: Dalia Bravo

Director of Content and Media Production:
Michael Burggren

Production Manager: Daisy Sosa

Media Researcher: Leila Hishmeh

Senior Print Buyer: Mary Beth Hennebury

Cover and Interior Designer:
Brenda Carmichael

Composition: Lumina

Cover Image: Hero Images/Getty Images

Bottom Images: (Left to Right) Jay B Sauceda/
Getty Images; Tripod/Getty Images;
Portra Images/Getty Images; Portra Images/
Getty Images; Mark Edward Atkinson/
Tracey Lee/Getty Images; James Porter/
Getty Images; Jade/Getty Images; Seth Joel/
Getty Images; LWA/Larry Williams/
Getty Images; Dimitri Otis/Getty Images

For product information and technology assistance, contact us at
Cengage Learning Customer & Sales Support, 1-800-354-9706

For permission to use material from this text or product,
submit all requests online at **cengage.com/permissions**

Further permissions questions can be emailed to
permissionrequest@cengage.com

Student Book
ISBN 13: 978-1-305-65552-2

National Geographic Learning/Cengage Learning
20 Channel Center Street
Boston, MA 02210
USA

Cengage Learning is a leading provider of customized learning solutions with office locations around the globe, including Singapore, the United Kingdom, Australia, Mexico, Brazil, and Japan. Locate your local office at:
international.cengage.com/region

Cengage Learning products are represented in Canada by Nelson Education, Ltd.

Visit National Geographic Learning online at **NGL.Cengage.com**
Visit our corporate website at **www.cengage.com**

Printed in Mexico
Quad / Graphics México.

Print Number: 04   Print Year: 2018

ACKNOWLEDGMENTS

Ellen Albano
Mcfatter Technical College, Davie, FL

Esther Anaya-Garcia
Glendale Community College, Glendale, AZ

Carol Bellamy
Prince George's Community College, Largo, MD

Gail Bier
Atlantic Technical College, Coconut Creek, FL

Kathryn Black
Myrtle Beach Family Learning Center, Myrtle Beach, SC

Claudia Brantley
College of Southern Nevada, Las Vegas, NV

Dr. Joan-Yvette Campbell
Lindsey Hopkins Technical College, Miami, FL

Maria Carmen Iglesias
Miami Senior Adult Educational Center, Miami, FL

Lee Chen
Palomar College, San Marcos, CA

Casey Cahill
Atlantic Technical College, Coconut Creek, FL

Maria Dillehay
Burien Job Training and Education Center, Goodwill, Seattle, WA

Irene Fjaerestad
Olympic College, Bremerton, WA

Eleanor Forfang-Brockman
Tarrant County College, Fort Worth, Texas

Jesse Galdamez
San Bernardino Adult School, San Bernardino, CA

Anna Garoz
Lindsey Hopkins Technical Education Center, Miami, FL

Maria Gutierrez
Miami Sunset Adult, Miami, FL

Noel Hernandez
Palm Beach County Public Schools, Palm Beach County, FL

Kathleen Hiscock
Portland Adult Education, Portland, ME

Frantz Jean-Louis
The English Center, Miami, FL

Annette Johnson
Sheridan Technical College, Hollywood, FL

Ginger Karaway
Gateway Technical College, Kenosha, WI

Judy Martin-Hall
Indian River State College, Fort Pierce, FL

Toni Molinaro
Dixie Hollins Adult Education Center, St Petersburg, FL

Tracey Person
Cape Cod Community College, Hyannis, MA

Celina Paula
Miami-Dade County Public Schools, Miami, FL

Veronica Pavon-Baker
Miami Beach Adult, Miami, FL

Ileana Perez
Robert Morgan Technical College, Miami, FL

Neeta Rancourt
Atlantic Technical College, Coconut Creek, FL

Brenda Roland
Joliet Junior College, Joliet, IL

Hidelisa Sampson
Las Vegas Urban League, Las Vegas, NV

Lisa Schick
James Madison University, Harrisonburg, VA

Rob Sheppard
Quincy Asian Resources, Quincy, MA

Sydney Silver
Burien Job Training and Education Center, Goodwill, Seattle, WA

Teresa Tamarit
Miami Senior Adult Educational Center, Miami, FL

Cristina Urena
Atlantic Technical College, Fort Lauderdale, FL

Pamela Jo Wilson
Palm Beach County Public Schools, Palm Beach County, FL

ABOUT THE AUTHORS

Staci Johnson

Ever since I can remember, I've been fascinated with other cultures and languages. I love to travel and every place I go, the first thing I want to do is meet the people, learn their language, and understand their culture. Becoming an ESL teacher was a perfect way to turn what I love to do into my profession. There's nothing more incredible than the exchange of teaching and learning from one another that goes on in an ESL classroom. And there's nothing more rewarding than helping a student succeed.

Rob Jenkins

I love teaching. I love to see the expressions on my students' faces when the light goes on and their eyes show such sincere joy of learning. I knew the first time I stepped into an ESL classroom that this is where I needed to be and I have never questioned that resolution. I have worked in business, sales, and publishing, and I've found challenge in all, but nothing can compare to the satisfaction of reaching people in such a personal way.

Along with the inclusion of National Geographic content, the third edition of **Stand Out** boasts of several innovations. In response to initiatives regarding the development of more complexity with reading and encouraging students to interact more with reading texts, we are proud to introduce new rich reading sections that allow students to discuss topics relevant to a global society. We have also introduced new National Geographic videos that complement the life-skill videos **Stand Out** introduced in the second edition and which are now integrated into the student books. We don't stop there; **Stand Out** has even more activities that require critical and creative thinking that serve to maximize learning and prepare students for the future. The third edition also has online workbooks. **Stand Out** was the first mainstream ESL textbook for adults to introduce a lesson plan format, hundreds of customizable worksheets, and project-based instruction. The third edition expands on these features in its mission to provide rich learning opportunities that can be exploited in different ways. We believe that with the innovative approach that made **Stand Out** a leader from its inception, the many new features, and the new look; programs, teachers, and students will find great success!

Stand Out Mission Statement:

Our goal is to give students challenging opportunities to be successful in their language learning experience so they develop confidence and become independent lifelong learners.

TO THE TEACHER

ABOUT THE SERIES

The **Stand Out** series is designed to facilitate *active* learning within life-skill settings that lead students to career and academic pathways. Each student book and its supplemental components in the six-level series expose students to competency areas most useful and essential for newcomers with careful treatment of level appropriate but challenging materials. Students grow academically by developing essential literacy and critical thinking skills that will help them find personal success in a changing and dynamic world.

THE STAND OUT PHILOSOPHY

Integrated Skills

In each of the five lessons of every unit, skills are introduced as they might be in real language use. They are in context and not separated into different sections of the unit. We believe that for real communication to occur, the classroom should mirror real-life as much as possible.

Objective Driven Activities

Every lesson in **Stand Out** is driven by a performance objective. These objectives have been carefully selected to ensure they are measurable, accessible to students at their particular level, and relevant to students and their lives. Good objectives lead to effective learning. Effective objectives also lead to appropriate self, student, and program assessment which is increasingly required by state and federal mandates.

Lesson Plan Sequencing

Stand Out follows an established sequence of activities that provides students with the tools they need to have in order to practice and apply the skills required in the objective. A pioneer in Adult Education for introducing the Madeline Hunter WIPPEA lesson plan model into textbooks, **Stand Out** continues to provide a clear and easy-to-follow system for presenting and developing English language skills. The WIPPEA model follows six steps:

- **W**arm up and Review
- **I**ntroduction
- **P**resentation
- **P**ractice
- **E**valuation
- **A**pplication

Learning And Acquisition

In **Stand Out**, the recycling of skills is emphasized. Students must learn and practice the same skills multiple times in various contexts to actually acquire them. Practicing a skill one time is rarely sufficient for acquisition and rarely addresses diverse student needs and learning styles.

Critical Thinking

Critical thinking has been defined in various ways and sometimes so broadly that any activity could be classified to meet the criteria. To be clear and to draw attention to the strong critical thinking activities in **Stand Out,** we define these activities as *tasks that require learners to think deeper than the superficial vocabulary and meaning.* Activities such as ranking, making predictions, analyzing, or solving problems, demand that students think beyond the surface. Critical thinking is highlighted throughout so the instructor can be confident that effective learning is going on.

Learner-Centered, Cooperative, and Communicative Activities

Stand Out provides ample opportunities for students to develop interpersonal skills and to practice new vocabulary through graphic organizers and charts like VENN diagrams, graphs, classifying charts, and mind maps. The lesson planners provide learner centered approaches in every lesson. Students are asked to rank items, make decisions, and negotiate amongst other things.

Dialogues are used to prepare students for these activities in the low levels and fewer dialogues are used at the higher levels where students have already acquired the vocabulary and rudimentary conversation skills.

Activities should provide opportunities for students to speak in near authentic settings so they have confidence to perform outside the classroom. This does not mean that dialogues and other mechanical activities are not used to prepare students for cooperative activities, but these mechanical activities do not foster conversation. They merely provide the first tools students need to go beyond mimicry.

Assessment

Instructors and students should have a clear understanding of what is being taught and what is expected. In **Stand Out**, objectives are clearly stated so that target skills can be effectively assessed throughout.

Formative assessments are essential. Pre and post-assessments can be given for units or sections of the book through *ExamView*—a program that makes developing tests easy and effective. These tests can be created to appear like standardized tests, which are important for funding and to help students prepare.

Finally, *learner logs* allow students to self-assess, document progress, and identify areas that might require additional attention.

SUPPLEMENTAL COMPONENTS

The **Stand Out** series is a comprehensive one-stop for all student needs. There is no need to look any further than the resources offered.

Stand Out Lesson Planners

The lesson planners go beyond merely describing activities in the student book by providing teacher support, ideas, and guidance for the entire class period.

- **Standards correlations** for **CCRS, CASAS,** and **SCANS** are identified for each lesson.
- **Pacing Guides** help with planning by giving instructors suggested durations for each activity and a selection of activities for different class lengths.
- **Teacher Tips** provide point-of-use pedagogical comments and best practices.
- **At-A-Glance Lesson Openers** provide the instructor with everything that will be taught in a particular lesson. Elements include: the agenda, the goal, grammar, pronunciation, academic strategies, critical thinking elements, correlations to standards, and resources.
- **Suggested Activities** go beyond what is shown in the text providing teachers with ideas that will stimulate them to come up with their own.
- **Listening Scripts** are integrated into the unit pages for easy access.

Stand Out Workbook

The workbook in the third edition takes the popular **Stand Out Grammar Challenge** and expands it to include vocabulary building, life-skill development, and grammar practice associated directly with each lesson in the student book.

Stand Out Online Workbook

One of the most important innovations new to the third edition of **Stand Out** is the online workbook. This workbook provides unique activities that are closely related to the student book and gives students opportunities to have access to audio and video.

The online workbook provides opportunities for students to practice and improve digital literacy skills essential for 21st century learners. These skills are essential for standardized computer and online testing. Scores in these tests will improve when students can concentrate on the content and not so much on the technology.

Activity Bank

The Activity Bank is an online feature that provides several hundred multilevel worksheets per level to enhance the already rich materials available through **Stand Out**.

DVD Program

The **Stand Out Lifeskills Video Program** continues to be available with eight episodes per level; however, now the worksheets are part of the student books with additional help in the lesson planners.

New to the third edition of **Stand Out** are two National Geographic videos per level. Each video is accompanied by four pages of instruction and activities with support in the lesson planners.

Examview

ExamView is a program that provides customizable test banks and allows instructors to make lesson, unit, and program tests quickly.

STANDARDS AND CORRELATIONS

Stand Out is the pioneer in establishing a foundation of standards within each unit and through every objective. The standards movement in the United States is as dominant today as it was when **Stand Out** was first published. Schools and programs must be aware of on-going local and federal initiatives and make attempts to meet ever-changing requirements.

In the first edition of **Stand Out**, we identified direct correlations to SCANS, EFF, and CASAS standards. *The Secretaries Commission on Achieving Necessary Skills* or SCANS and *Equipped for the Future* or EFF standards are still important and are identified in every lesson of **Stand Out**. These skills include the basic skills, interpersonal skills, and problem-solving skills necessary to be successful in the workplace, in school, and in the community. **Stand Out** was also developed with a thorough understanding of objectives established by the *Comprehensive Adult Student Assessment Systems* or CASAS. Many programs have experienced great success with their CASAS scores using **Stand Out**, and these objectives continue to be reflected in the third edition.

Today, a new emphasis on critical thinking and complexity has swept the nation. Students are expected to think for themselves more now than ever before. They must also interact with reading texts at a higher level. These new standards and expectations are highly visible in the third edition and include *College and Career Readiness Standards.*

Stand Out offers a complete set of correlations online for all standards to demonstrate how closely we align with state and federal guidelines.

IMPORTANT INNOVATIONS TO THE THIRD EDITION

New Look
Although the third edition of **Stand Out** boasts of the same lesson plan format and task-based activities that made it one of the most popular books in adult education, it now has an updated look with the addition of the National Geographic content which will capture the attention of the instructor and every student.

Critical Thinking
With the advent of new federal and state initiatives, teachers need to be confident that students will use critical thinking skills when learning. This has always been a goal in **Stand Out**, but now those opportunities are highlighted in each lesson.

College And Career Readiness Skills
These skills are also identified by critical thinking strategies and academic-related activities, which are found throughout **Stand Out**. New to the third edition is a special reading section in each unit that challenges students and encourages them to develop reading strategies within a rich National Geographic environment.

Stand Out Workbook
The print workbook is now more extensive and complete with vocabulary, life skills, and grammar activities to round out any program. Many instructors might find these pages ideal for homework, but they of course can be used for additional practice within the classroom.

Media And Online Support
Media and online support includes audio, video, online workbooks, presentation tools, and multi-level worksheets, ExamView, and standards correlations.

CONTENTS

Numeracy/ Academic Skills	CCRS	SCANS	CASAS
• Writing a paragraph • Comparing and contrasting • Setting goals	RI1, RI3, RI7 W2, W3, W4 SL1, SL2, SL3 L2, L5	**Many SCAN skills are incorporated in this unit with an emphasis on:** • Understanding systems • Decision making	**1:** 0.1.2; 0.1.4; 0.2.1; 0.2.2 **2:** 0.2.1; 7.2.6 **3:** 0.1.2, 0.1.6, 0.2.1, 7.1.1
• Pronunciation • Reading a chart • Active reading • Focused listening • Writing a paragraph • Making inferences • Using an outline • Using a pie graph • Reviewing	RI1, RI2, RI4, RI7 W4, W5 SL1, SL2, SL4 L1, L2, L3, L4	**Many SCAN skills are incorporated in this unit with an emphasis on:** • Allocating time • Understanding systems • Applying technology to task • Responsibility • Self management • Writing • Decision making	**1:** 0.1.2, 0.2.4 **2:** 7.1.1, 7.1.2, 7.1.3, 7.2.5, 7.2.6 **3:** 7.1.1, 7.1.2, 7.1.3, 7.2.5, 7.2.6 **4:** 0.1.5, 7.4.1, 7.4.3, 7.4.5 **5:** 7.4.2 **R:** 7.2.1 **TP:** 4.8.1., 4.8.5., 4.8.6.
• Pronunciation: Stress • Test taking skills • Comparing and contrasting • Sequence writing • Reviewing	RI1, RI2, RI4, RI5, RI7 W2, W4 SL1, SL2, SL4 L1, L2, L3, L5	**Many SCAN skills are incorporated in this unit with an emphasis on:** • Responsibility • Participating as a member of a team • Acquiring and evaluating information • Organizing and maintaining information • Decision making • Reasoning	**1:** 0.1.2, 1.3.7 **2:** 1.2.1 **3:** 1.2.1, 1.2.2 **4:** 1.3.1 **5:** 1.2.5 **R:** 7.2.1 **TP:** 4.8.1., 4.8.5., 4.8.6.

CONTENTS

Numeracy/ Academic Skills	CCRS	SCANS	CASAS
• Pronunciation: Rising and falling intonation • Scanning • Active reading • Focused listening • Reading a bar graph • Budget arithmetic • Writing a business letter • Reviewing	RI1, RI2, RI3, RI4, RI5, RI7, RI8 W1, W4, W5 SL1, SL2, SL4 L1, L2, L3, L5	**Many SCAN skills are incorporated in this unit with an emphasis on:** • Allocating money • Understanding systems • Monitoring and correcting performance • Interpreting and communicating information • Reading • Writing • Decision making	**1:** 1.4.1, 1.4.2 **2:** 1.4.2, 7.2.7 **3:** 1.4.4, 1.5.3 **4:** 1.5.1, 6.0.3, 6.0.5, 6.1.1, 6.1.2 **5:** 1.4.7 **R:** 7.2.1 **TP:** 4.8.1, 4.8.5, 4.8.6.
• Pronunciation: Rising and falling intonation • Pronunciation: Phrasing • Focused listening • Making inferences • Reading charts • Reading a map • Paragraph writing • Reviewing	RI1, RI2, RI3, RI4, RI5, RI6, RI7 W1, W2, W4, W5 SL1, SL2, SL3, SL4 L1, L2, L3, L5	**Many SCAN skills are incorporated in this unit with an emphasis on:** • Understanding systems • Interpreting and communicating information • Writing • Decision making • Seeing things in the mind's eye	**1:** 0.1.2 **2:** 1.8.5, 2.5.6 **3:** 2.2.1, 2.2.5 **4:** 7.2.6 **5:** 7.2.2 **R:** 7.2.1 **TP:** 4.8.1, 4.8.5, 4.8.6
• Active listening • Active reading • Reviewing	R1, R2, R3, R4, R7 W2, W7 SL1, SL2, SL3, SL4 L1, L2, L3, L4	**Many SCAN skills are incorporated in this unit with an emphasis on:** • Understanding systems • Self management • Acquiring and evaluating information • Interpreting and communicating information	**1:** 3.1.1, 3.1.3, 3.2.1 **2:** 3.1.1 **3:** 3.4.2, 3.5.9 **4:** 3.5.1, 3.5.3, 3.5.5, 3.5.9, 6.7.3 **5:** 3.5.9 **R:** 7.2.1 **TP:** 4.8.1, 4.8.5, 4.8.6.

CONTENTS

Numeracy/ Academic Skills	CCRS	SCANS	CASAS
• Paragraph writing • Reading for understanding • Focused listening • Reviewing	RI1, RI2, RI3, RI4, RI7 W1, W4, W5, W8 SL1, SL2, SL3, SL4, SL6 L1, L2, L3, L5	**Many SCAN skills are incorporated in this unit with an emphasis on:** • Self-esteem • Sociability • Acquiring and evaluating information • Speaking • Decision making	**1:** 4.1.8 **2:** 4.1.9 **3:** 4.1.3 **4:** 4.1.2 **5:** 4.1.5, 4.1.7 **R:** 7.2.1 **TP:** 4.8.1, 4.8.5, 4.8.6.
• Pronunciation: Rising intonation for polite requests • Pronunciation: Tone of voice • Focused listening • Reading for understanding	RI1, RI2, RI3, RI4, RI7, RI8 W1, W2, W4, W5, W7, W8 SL1, SL2, Sl3, SL4 L1, L2, L3, L5	**Many SCAN skills are incorporated in this unit with an emphasis on:** • Understanding systems • Participating as a member of a team • Acquiring and evaluating	**1:** 4.1.9, 4.4.1 **2:** 4.2.1, 4.4.3 **3:** 4.2.1 **4:** 4.3.3, 4.3.4, 4.5.1 **5:** 4.4.1, 4.6.1 **R:** 7.2.1 **TP:** 4.8.1, 4.8.5, 4.8.6
• Focused listening • Active reading • Paragraph writing • Speech writing • Reviewing	RI1, RI2, RI3, RI4, RI5, RI6, RI7, RI8 W1, W4, W5, W9 SL1, SL2, SL3, SL4, SL6 L1, L2, L3, L5	**Many SCAN skills are incorporated in this unit with an emphasis on:** • Listening • Speaking • Responsibility • Self-esteem	**1:** 5.1.6 **2:** 5.1.4, 5.1.6 **3:** 5.1.4, 5.2.1 **4:** 5.5.7, 5.5.8 **5:** 5.1.6 **R:** 7.2.1 **TP:** 4.8.1, 4.8.5, 4.8.6.

Appendices

For other national and state specific standards, please visit: **www.NGL.Cengage.com/SO3**

INTRODUCING
STAND OUT, Third Edition!

Stand Out is a six-level, standards-based ESL series for adult education with a proven track record of successful results. The new edition of *Stand Out* continues to provide students with the foundations and tools needed to achieve success in life, college, and career.

Stand Out now integrates real-world content from National Geographic

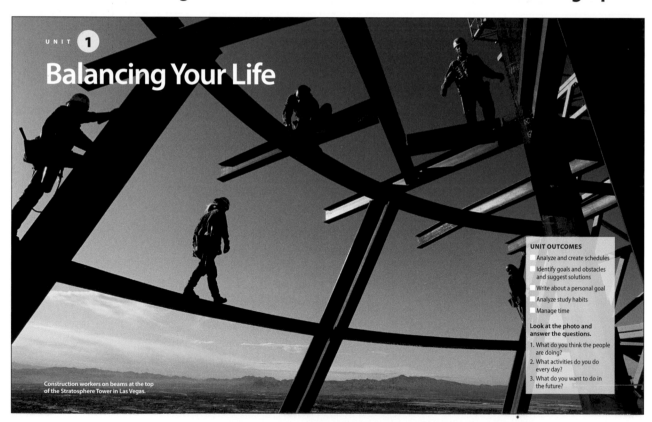

UNIT **1**
Balancing Your Life

UNIT OUTCOMES

- Analyze and create schedules
- Identify goals and obstacles and suggest solutions
- Write about a personal goal
- Analyze study habits
- Manage time

Look at the photo and answer the questions.

1. What do you think the people are doing?
2. What activities do you do every day?
3. What do you want to do in the future?

Construction workers on beams at the top of the Stratosphere Tower in Las Vegas.

- *Stand Out* now integrates high-interest, real-world content from National Geographic which enhances its proven approach to lesson planning and instruction. A stunning National Geographic image at the beginning of each unit introduces the theme and engages learners in meaningful conversations right from the start.

Stand Out supports college and career readiness

Carefully crafted activities help prepare students for college and career success.

- **NEW Reading Challenge** in every unit features a fascinating story about a **National Geographic explorer** to immerse learners in authentic content.

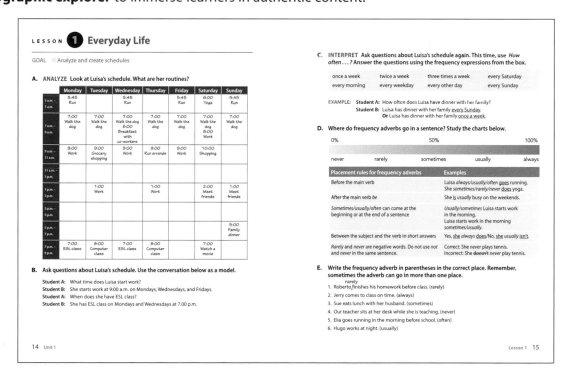

- **EXPANDED Critical Thinking Activities** challenge learners to evaluate, analyze, and synthesize information to prepare them for the workplace and academic life.

- **NEW Video Challenge** showcases **National Geographic footage and explorers**, providing learners with the opportunity to synthesize what they have learned in prior units through the use of authentic content.

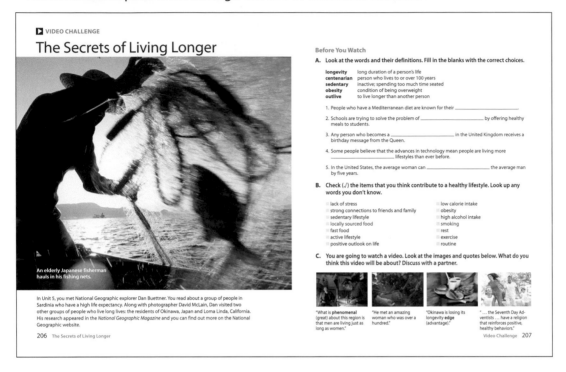

▶ VIDEO CHALLENGE

The Secrets of Living Longer

An elderly Japanese fisherman hauls in his fishing nets.

In Unit 5, you met National Geographic explorer Dan Buettner. You read about a group of people in Sardinia who have a high life expectancy. Along with photographer David McLain, Dan visited two other groups of people who live long lives: the residents of Okinawa, Japan and Loma Linda, California. His research appeared in the *National Geographic Magazine* and you can find out more on the National Geographic website.

206   The Secrets of Living Longer

Before You Watch

A. Look at the words and their definitions. Fill in the blanks with the correct choices.

longevity	long duration of a person's life
centenarian	person who lives to or over 100 years
sedentary	inactive; spending too much time seated
obesity	condition of being overweight
outlive	to live longer than another person

1. People who have a Mediterranean diet are known for their _____

2. Schools are trying to solve the problem of _____ by offering healthy meals to students.

3. Any person who becomes a _____ in the United Kingdom receives a birthday message from the Queen.

4. Some people believe that the advances in technology mean people are living more _____ lifestyles than ever before.

5. In the United States, the average woman can _____ the average man by five years.

B. Check (✓) the items that you think contribute to a healthy lifestyle. Look up any words you don't know.

▢ lack of stress	▢ low calorie intake
▢ strong connections to friends and family	▢ obesity
▢ sedentary lifestyle	▢ high alcohol intake
▢ locally sourced food	▢ smoking
▢ fast food	▢ rest
▢ active lifestyle	▢ exercise
▢ positive outlook on life	▢ routine

C. You are going to watch a video. Look at the images and quotes below. What do you think this video will be about? Discuss with a partner.

"What is **phenomenal** (great) about this region is that men are living just as long as women."

"He met an amazing woman who was over a hundred."

"Okinawa is losing its longevity **edge** (advantage)."

"... the Seventh Day Adventists ... have a religion that reinforces positive, healthy behaviors."

Video Challenge   207

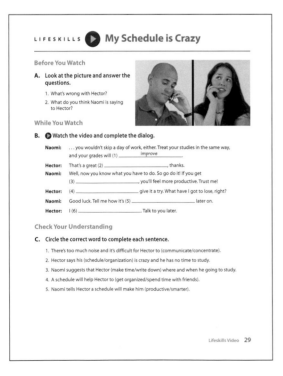

LIFESKILLS ▶ **My Schedule is Crazy**

Before You Watch

A. Look at the picture and answer the questions.

1. What's wrong with Hector?
2. What do you think Naomi is saying to Hector?

While You Watch

B. ▶ Watch the video and complete the dialog.

Naomi: . . . you wouldn't skip a day of work, either. Treat your studies in the same way, and your grades will (1) ___improve___

Hector: That's a great (2) _____ thanks.

Naomi: Well, now you know what you have to do. So go do it! If you get (3) _____, you'll feel more productive. Trust me!

Hector: (4) _____ give it a try. What have I got to lose, right?

Naomi: Good luck. Tell me how it's (5) _____ later on.

Hector: I (6) _____. Talk to you later.

Check Your Understanding

C. Circle the correct word to complete each sentence.

1. There's too much noise and it's difficult for Hector to (communicate/concentrate).
2. Hector says his (schedule/organization) is crazy and he has no time to study.
3. Naomi suggests that Hector (make time/write down) where and when he going to study.
4. A schedule will help Hector to (get organized/spend time with friends).
5. Naomi tells Hector a schedule will make him (productive/smarter).

Lifeskills Video   29

- The **Lifeskills Video** is a dramatic video series integrated into each unit of the student book that helps students learn natural spoken English and apply it to their everyday activities.

Pages shown are from *Stand Out*, Third Edition Level 3

- **NEW Online Workbook** engages students and supports the classroom by providing a wide variety of auto-graded interactive activities, an audio program, video from National Geographic, and pronunciation activities.

- **UPDATED Lesson Planner** includes correlations to **College and Career Readiness Standards (CCRS)**, **CASAS, SCANS** and reference to **EL Civics** competencies to help instructors achieve the required standards.

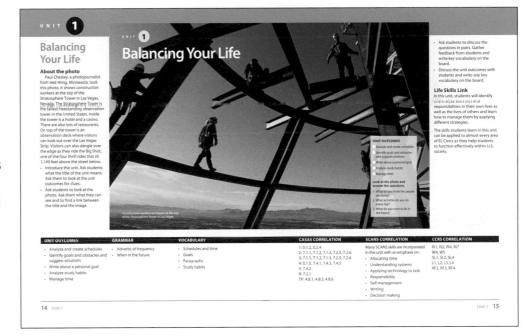

- **Teacher support** *Stand Out* continues to provide a wide variety of user-friendly tools and interactive activities that help teachers prepare students for success while keeping them engaged and motivated.

Stand Out supports teachers and learners

LEARNER COMPONENTS

- Student Book
- Online workbook powered by My**ELT**
- Print workbook

TEACHER COMPONENTS

- Lesson Planner
- Classroom DVD
- Assessment CD-ROM
- Teacher's companion site with Multi-Level Worksheets

Getting to Know You

UNIT OUTCOMES

- Introduce yourself and greet others
- Write about yourself
- Identify goals

GOAL ■ Introduce yourself and greet others

A. Complete the school registration form.

SANTA ANA ADULT SCHOOL
REGISTRATION FORM

First Name _____ Middle Initial _____

Last Name _____

Address:
Number and Street _____

City _____ State _____ Zip _____

Phone:
Home _____ Cell _____

E-mail Address _____

Date of Birth (mm/dd/yyyy) _____ / _____ / _____

Languages Spoken _____

Occupation _____

B. FIND OUT Write three questions to ask your classmates about the information on their registration forms.

1. _____

2. _____

3. _____

C. SURVEY Write your questions from Exercise B in the table and interview two classmates. Use the conversations below as models.

You:	What is your <u>first name</u>?
Student A:	My first name is Michel.
You:	What's your <u>first name</u>?
Student B:	My first name is Selma.

CONTRACTIONS

What is = *What's*

What's your name?

Question	Student A	Student B

D. Introduce the two classmates you interviewed to the rest of the class.

EXAMPLE: This is Michel. His last name is Caron. He is from Haiti.
This is Selma. Her last name is Bezerra. She's from Brazil.

E. **Juan and Michel take English class together. Read and practice their conversation.**

Juan:	Good morning.
Michel:	Morning!
Juan:	How are you today?
Michel:	Great! How about you?
Juan:	Fine, thanks.

 F. **Listen to the greetings and possible responses.**

CD 1
TR 1

Greetings	Possible Responses
Hi!	Hello!
Good morning!	Morning!
How are you today?	Fine. / Great!
How's it going?	Pretty good.
How are you doing?	OK. / Not bad.
What's up?	Nothing.
What's new?	Not much.

G. **Listen to the greetings and respond after each one.**

CD 1
TR 2

H. **APPLY** **Greet three different classmates. Ask them a few personal information questions like the ones you wrote in Exercise B.**

There are many different ways to accompany a greeting. In the United States, the most common is a handshake.

LESSON ❷ Tell your story

GOAL ■ Write about yourself

A. Read about Akiko.

My name is Akiko Sugiyama. I'm a student at Santa Ana Adult School. I came to the United States five years ago from Japan with my husband and three children. We live in Santa Ana, California. My husband works in a computer assembly factory. I go to school and take care of our children. We are both studying English because we want to be successful in this country. Someday we hope to buy a house and send our children to college.

B. RESTATE Answer the questions about Akiko.

1. When did Akiko come to the United States? _____

2. Where is she from? _____

3. Who did she come to the United States with? _____

4. Where does she live? _____

5. What does her husband do? _____

6. What does she do? _____

7. Why is she studying English? _____

8. What are her future goals? _____

C. Answer the questions about yourself.

1. When did you come to this country? _____

2. Where are you from? _____

3. Who did you come to this country with? _____

4. Where do you live? _____

5. What do you do? _____

6. Why are you studying English? _____

7. What are your future goals? _____

D. ANALYZE Study the layout of the paragraph.

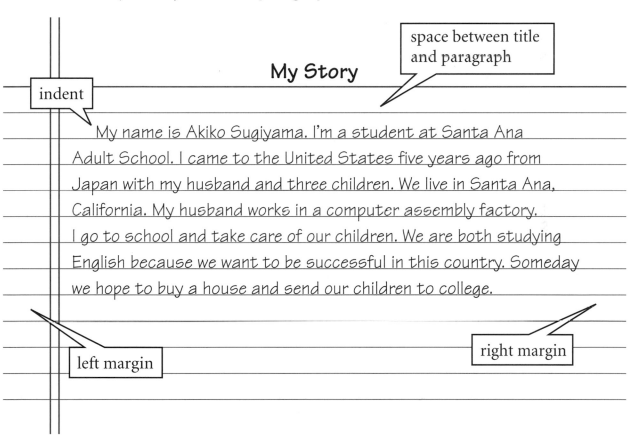

E. COMPOSE Write a paragraph about yourself with the answers you wrote in Exercise C. Use correct paragraph formatting like in Akiko's paragraph in Exercise D.

F. COMPARE Share your paragraph with a partner. Did your partner use correct paragraph formatting like in Akiko's paragraph?

LESSON ③ Are you college bound?

GOAL ▇ Identify goals

A. This pyramid represents the educational system in the United States. Read the pyramid with your teacher.

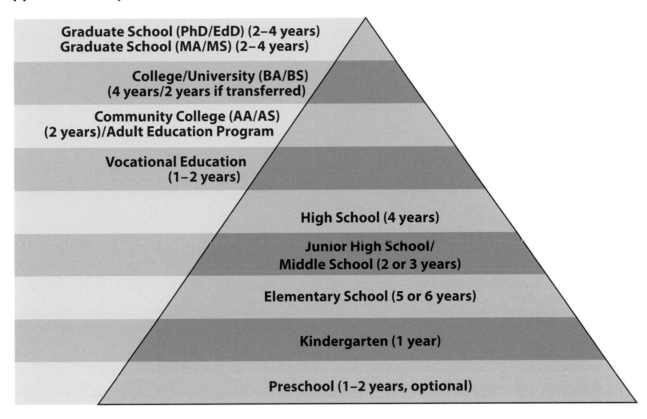

Graduate School (PhD/EdD) (2–4 years)
Graduate School (MA/MS) (2–4 years)

College/University (BA/BS)
(4 years/2 years if transferred)

Community College (AA/AS)
(2 years)/Adult Education Program

Vocational Education
(1–2 years)

High School (4 years)

Junior High School/
Middle School (2 or 3 years)

Elementary School (5 or 6 years)

Kindergarten (1 year)

Preschool (1–2 years, optional)

B. **PREDICT** What do the abbreviations in the table stand for and mean? Ask your teacher for help.

Abbreviation	Stands for . . .	Meaning
AA	Associate of Arts	two-year degree from a community college with an art-related major
AS		
MA		
MS		
PhD		
EdD		

C. **Choose the best answer. Look back at the pyramid if you need help.**

1. What is the lowest level of education in the United States?

   a. kindergarten   b. preschool   c. graduate school

2. How many years do students go to high school?

   a. three years   b. two years   c. four years

3. What is the highest degree you can get?

   a. MA   b. MS   c. PhD

4. Where can you get a BA or BS degree?

   a. college   b. graduate school   c. technical college

D. **COMPARE** Use the pyramid below to show your country's educational system. Compare your pyramid with a classmate's.

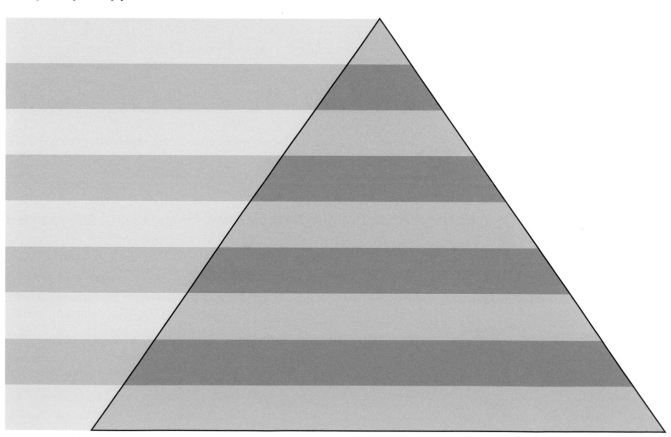

E. Check (✓) the educational levels you have completed. Circle the educational level you would like to achieve.

Graduate School (PhD/EdD) (2–4 years)
Graduate School (MA/MS) (2–4 years)

College/University (BA/BS)
(4 years/2 years if transferred)

Community College (AA/AS)
(2 years)/Adult Education Program

Vocational Education
(1–2 years)

High School (4 years)

Junior High School/
Middle School (2 or 3 years)

Elementary School (5 or 6 years)

Kindergarten (1 year)

Preschool (1–2 years, optional)

F. **COMPOSE** How do you plan to achieve your educational goals? Write a paragraph.

_____

_____

_____

_____

_____

_____

_____

_____

_____

Balancing Your Life

Construction workers balance on beams at the
top of the Stratosphere Tower in Las Vegas.

UNIT OUTCOMES

- Analyze and create schedules
- Identify goals and obstacles and suggest solutions
- Write about a personal goal
- Analyze study habits
- Manage time

Look at the photo and answer the questions.

1. What do you think the people are doing?

2. What activities do you do every day?

3. What do you want to do in the future?

GOAL ■ Analyze and create schedules

A. ANALYZE Look at Luisa's schedule. What are her routines?

	Monday	Tuesday	Wednesday	Thursday	Friday	Saturday	Sunday
5 a.m. – 7 a.m.	5:45 Run		5:45 Run		5:45 Run	6:00 Yoga	5:45 Run
7 a.m. – 9 a.m.	7:00 Walk the dog	7:00 Walk the dog	7:00 Walk the dog 8:00 Breakfast with co-workers	7:00 Walk the dog	7:00 Walk the dog	7:00 Walk the dog 8:00 Work	7:00 Walk the dog
9 a.m. – 11 a.m.	9:00 Work	9:00 Grocery shopping	9:00 Work	9:00 Run errands	9:00 Work	10:00 Shopping	
11 a.m. – 1 p.m.							
1 p.m. – 3 p.m.		1:00 Work		1:00 Work		2:00 Meet friends	1:00 Meet friends
3 p.m. – 5 p.m.							
5 p.m. – 7 p.m.							5:00 Family dinner
7 p.m. – 9 p.m.	7:00 ESL class	8:00 Computer class	7:00 ESL class	8:00 Computer class		7:00 Watch a movie	

B. Ask questions about Luisa's schedule. Use the conversation below as a model.

Student A: What time does Luisa start work?

Student B: She starts work at 9:00 a.m. on Mondays, Wednesdays, and Fridays.

Student A: When does she have ESL class?

Student B: She has ESL class on Mondays and Wednesdays at 7:00 p.m.

C. **INTERPRET** Ask questions about Luisa's schedule again. This time, use *How often . . . ?* Answer the questions using the frequency expressions from the box.

once a week	twice a week	three times a week	every Saturday
every morning	every weekday	every other day	every Sunday

EXAMPLE: **Student A:** How often does Luisa have dinner with her family?
Student B: Luisa has dinner with her family <u>every Sunday</u>.
Or Luisa has dinner with her family <u>once a week</u>.

D. Where do frequency adverbs go in a sentence? Study the charts below.

0%   50%   100%

never   rarely   sometimes   usually   always

Placement rules for frequency adverbs	Examples
Before the main verb	Luisa *always/usually/often* <u>goes</u> running. She *sometimes/rarely/never* <u>does</u> yoga.
After the main verb *be*	She <u>is</u> *usually* busy on the weekends.
Sometimes/usually/often can come at the beginning or at the end of a sentence	*Usually/sometimes* Luisa starts work in the morning. Luisa starts work in the morning *sometimes/usually*.
Between the subject and the verb in short answers	Yes, <u>she</u> *always* <u>does</u>./No, <u>she</u> *usually* <u>isn't</u>.
Rarely and *never* are negative words. Do not use *not* and *never* in the same sentence.	Correct: She *never* plays tennis. Incorrect: She ~~doesn't~~ *never* play tennis.

E. Write the frequency adverb in parentheses in the correct place. Remember, sometimes the adverb can go in more than one place.

      rarely
1. Roberto ⌃ finishes his homework before class. (rarely)

2. Jerry comes to class on time. (always)

3. Sue eats lunch with her husband. (sometimes)

4. Our teacher sits at her desk while she is teaching. (never)

5. Elia goes running in the morning before school. (often)

6. Hugo works at night. (usually)

F. Use frequency adverbs to write sentences about Luisa. Look back at her schedule in Exercise A.

1. _Luisa usually starts work in the morning._ _____

2. _____

3. _____

4. _____

G. Practice reading the sentences you wrote in Exercise F. Which words are the most important in each sentence?

H. **CREATE** Make a schedule of everything you do in one week. Tell your partner about your schedule.

EXAMPLE: I NEVER cook on my day off because I'm a cook in a restaurant!

STRESS

In a phrase or sentence, certain words get the most stress. In the sentences below, the words with the most stress are in CAPITAL letters.

Luisa OFTEN goes RUNNING.

She is NEVER HOME on the weekends.

SOMETIMES I go to the MOVIES.

He RARELY studies in the MORNING.

	Monday	Tuesday	Wednesday	Thursday	Friday	Saturday	Sunday
5 a.m. – 7 a.m.							
7 a.m. – 9 a.m.							
9 a.m. – 11 a.m.							
11 a.m. – 1 p.m.							
1 p.m. – 3 p.m.							
3 p.m. – 5 p.m.							
5 p.m. – 7 p.m.							
7 p.m. – 9 p.m.							

LESSON ② Goals, obstacles, and solutions

GOAL ▪ Identify goals and obstacles and suggest solutions

A. Look at the picture. Zhou is worried about the future. What is he thinking about?

B. Read about Zhou.

> Zhou's life is going to change very soon. His wife, Huixen, is going to have twins in July. His parents are going to come from China to live in the United States. He's happy, but his apartment will to be too small for everyone. He needs a better job, but his boss *won't* promote him because he doesn't have a college degree.
>
> Zhou has three goals. When his parents come to the United States, he will buy a house large enough for two families. His father will work and help pay for the house. His mother will help take care of the children. Then, Zhou plans to go to night school and get his bachelor's degree. When he graduates, he will apply for a new position at work. He will work hard to achieve his goals.
>
> *won't = will not

C. A *goal* is something you would like to achieve in the future. What are Zhou's three goals?

1. _____

2. _____

3. _____

D. An *obstacle* is a problem; something that gets in the way of your goal. Zhou has two obstacles. What are they?

1. _____

2. _____

E. Review vocabulary and write about Zhou's solutions.

1. What is a goal? _____

2. What is an obstacle? _____

3. What is a solution? _A solution is a way to solve a problem._____

4. Zhou's apartment is too small. What is his solution?

   _____

5. Zhou needs a better job. What is his solution?

   _____

F. IDENTIFY Listen to Tuba and Lam. Identify their goals, obstacles, and solutions and write them in the spaces.

CD 1
TR 3

1. **Goal:** Tuba wants to _get a job to help her husband_____.

   Obstacle: Her obstacle is _____.

   Solutions:

   a. She can _____.

   b. Her mother can _____.

2. **Goal:** Lam wants to _____.

   Obstacle: His obstacle is _____.

   Solutions:

   a. His grandchildren can _____.

   b. His grandchildren can _____.

G. Read how to use *when* to talk about goals.

1. *When* Zhou *graduates*, he *will* apply for a new position at work.

   This sentence means: *First,* he will graduate. *Then,* he will apply for a new position at work.

2. *When* his parents *come* to the United States, he *will* buy a house.

   This sentence means: *First,* his parents will come to the United States. *Then,* he will buy a house.

H. Study the chart.

Future Time Clauses with *When*			
When	**Present tense**	*Will*	**Base verb**
When Zhou	graduates,	he will	apply for a new position at work.*
When his parents	come to the United States,	he will	buy a house.

*Note: The order of the clauses does not matter. You can also say, *Zhou will apply for a new position at work when he graduates.*

I. Complete the sentences below with your own ideas.

1. When Zhou's parents come to the United States, _his house will be too small_____.

2. When _____, they will buy a bigger house.

3. When Zhou's mother comes to stay, _____.

4. When _____, his boss will promote him.

5. When Zhou gets a better job, _____.

J. CLASSIFY Zhou has a *personal* goal (buy a new home), an *educational* goal (graduate from college), and an *occupational* goal (get a new position at work). **What are your goals? Write them in the table below.**

Personal	Educational	Occupational
1. _____	1. _____	1. _____
2. _____	2. _____	2. _____
3. _____	3. _____	3. _____

K. In groups, discuss your goals for the future.

EXAMPLE: When I graduate, I will get a new job.

L. APPLY Write your goals on a separate piece of paper. Hang it up in the classroom where you can read your goals each day.

LESSON ③ The future

GOAL ◼ Write about a personal goal

A. **Complete the paragraph below with *obstacles* and *solutions*.**

   In the previous lesson, you wrote about your goals. Goals are things you want to achieve. Sometimes we can have problems achieving them. These problems are called _____. When we figure out how to solve these problems, we have _____.

B. **ANALYZE** **Choose one of the goals you wrote in the table on page 19. Think of one obstacle to reaching your goal and two possible solutions.**

   Goal: _____

   Obstacle: _____

   Solutions:

   1. _____

   _____

   _____

   2. _____

   _____

   _____

C. **Share your ideas with a partner. Can your partner suggest other solutions?**

D. **What is a paragraph? Discuss the following terms with your teacher.**

   • A *paragraph* is a group of sentences about the same topic.

   • A *topic sentence* is usually the first sentence in a paragraph and it introduces the topic or *main idea*.

   • *Support sentences* are the sentences that follow the topic sentence and they give *details* about the topic.

   • A *conclusion sentence* is the final sentence of the paragraph and it gives a *summary* of the paragraph.

E. Read the paragraph Tuba wrote about her goal.

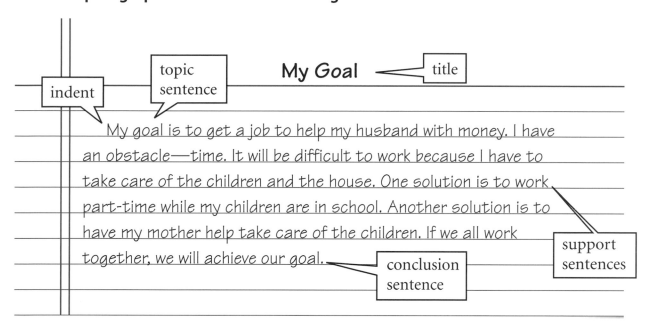

indent | topic sentence | **My Goal** ← title

    My goal is to get a job to help my husband with money. I have
an obstacle—time. It will be difficult to work because I have to
take care of the children and the house. One solution is to work
part-time while my children are in school. Another solution is to
have my mother help take care of the children. If we all work
together, we will achieve our goal.

support sentences

conclusion sentence

Malala Yousafzai's personal goal is to give children and young people around the world equal rights.

F. **ANALYZE** Look again at Tuba's paragraph in Exercise E and answer the questions. Then, write ideas for your own paragraph about the goal you chose in Exercise B.

1. What is Tuba's topic sentence?

_____

_____

_____

_____

2. Tuba's support sentences are about her obstacle and her two possible solutions. What are her support sentences?

_____

_____

_____

_____

_____

_____

3. What is Tuba's conclusion sentence?

_____

_____

_____

_____

1. Write your topic sentence.

_____

_____

_____

_____

2. Write your three support sentences.

a. _____

_____

b. _____

_____

c. _____

_____

3. Write your conclusion sentence.

_____

_____

_____

_____

G. On a separate piece of paper, write a paragraph about your goal using correct paragraph formatting.

LESSON **4** Study habits

GOAL ▪ Analyze study habits

A. Answer the following questions. Then, compare your answers with a partner.

1. Where do you like to study?

_____

2. When do you usually study?

_____

3. How long do you study for?

_____

4. Do you listen to music when you study? Why or why not?

_____

_____

B. **COMPARE** Look at the first picture. What is Luisa doing? Do you think she is learning anything? Why or why not? Look at the second picture. What is Michel doing? Is he learning anything? Discuss your ideas with a partner.

C. Listen to the information about study habits and take notes. What are good and bad study habits?

_____

_____

_____

_____

D. Read about study habits below.

Good study habits can be very *beneficial* to you and your education. On the other hand, bad study habits can be *harmful* to your educational goals. First, let's talk about bad study habits.

Many people have very busy schedules and it is difficult for them to find time to study. One bad study habit is not studying before class. Another bad study habit is studying with *distractions* around, such as television, people talking, or loud music. A third bad study habit is copying a friend's homework. These are just a few bad study habits, but you can easily change them into good study habits.

There are many ways that you can improve your study habits. First, set a time every day to study and try to study at the same time every day. Do not make appointments at this time. This is your special study time. Second, find a good place to study, a place that is quiet and comfortable so you can *concentrate*. Finally, do your homework on your own. Afterwards, you can find a friend to help you *go over* your work and check your answers.

E. INTERPRET According to the reading, what are some bad study habits? Add one more idea.

not studying before class
_____
_____
_____

F. INTERPRET According to the reading, what are some good study habits? Add one more idea.

studying at the same time every day
_____
_____
_____

G. **Match each word or phrase with its correct definition. Write the letter.**

1. _____ beneficial   a. bad for you

2. _____ harmful   b. get better

3. _____ distractions   c. review or check again

4. _b_ improve   d. good for you

5. _____ concentrate   e. think hard about something

6. _____ go over   f. things that disturb your studying

H. **Fill in the blanks with a word or phrase from Exercise G.**

1. My English will _____ if I practice every day.

2. Please be quiet. I can't _____ on my homework.

3. Studying with a friend can be _____ because you can help each other.

4. When you finish taking a test, _____ your answers again.

5. It's hard to study when there are _____. Turn off the TV!

6. Bad study habits can be _____ to your educational goals.

I. **Choose three words or phrases from Exercise G and write sentences about your study habits on a separate piece of paper. Share your sentences with a partner.**

J. **Think about your study habits. Fill in the table below.**

Good study habits	Bad study habits
1.	1.
2.	2.
3.	3.

K. **COMPARE** Share your answers with a partner. Which study habits are the same? Which study habits are different?

GOAL ■ Manage time

A. Read about Lara's problem.

> Lara doesn't spend enough time with her family. The pie chart shows how Lara spends her time. She rarely has any free time to relax. Lara wants to find a way to balance her time, so she has decided to attend a lecture at school to learn better time-management strategies.

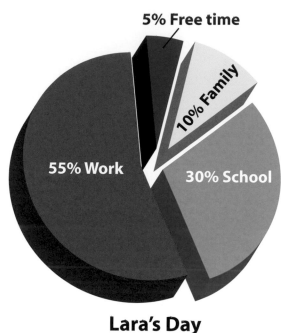

5% Free time

10% Family

55% Work

30% School

Lara's Day

B. Answer the questions about Lara.

1. What is Lara's goal?

_____

2. What is her obstacle?

_____

3. What is her solution?

_____

CD 1
TR 5
C. Listen to the lecture about time management. Listen for the main ideas.

Drivers in Los Angeles spend a lot of time going to and coming home from work because of traffic.

D. DISCUSS When you listen to a lecture, you can use an outline to help record important information. Look at the outline below and discuss it with your teacher.

1. Why is time management important?

   a. You stay organized.

   b. You accomplish everything that needs to get done.

   c. You _____.

2. How do you keep a schedule?

   a. Write down everything you need to do in a week.

   b. Put each task in a time slot.

   c. _____.

   d. Check off things that have been completed.

3. How can you add more time to your day?

   a. You can wake up earlier.

   b. You can ask _____.

   c. You can try doing _____ tasks at once.

4. What are other important things to consider about time management?

   a. Remember the important people in your life.

   b. _____

   c. You are the boss of your schedule.

5. What are the benefits of managing your time?

   a. You will have more time.

   b. You will feel less _____.

   c. You will have time to _____.

🎧 **E.** Listen to the lecture on time management again and complete the outline above.

CD 1
TR 5

F. A pie chart is a circle, like a pie, and is divided up into parts that equal 100%. Look at the pie chart, fill in the percentages below, and add them up. Do they equal 100%?

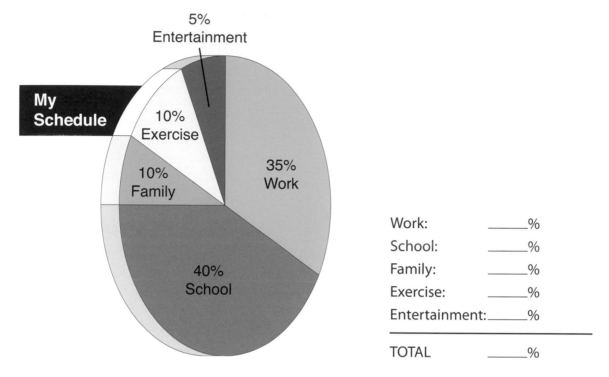

Work: _____%

School: _____%

Family: _____%

Exercise: _____%

Entertainment:_____%

_____

TOTAL _____%

G. On a separate piece of paper, create a pie chart to show how you spend your time. Make sure your chart equals 100%!

H. **REFLECT** Answer the following questions about your own time-management strategies.

1. What problems do you have with time?

   I work ten hours a day, and I don't have time to study.

   _____

2. How could you add more time to your day? (Think about what you learned from the lecture.)

   _____

   _____

3. What are some time-management skills you learned that you would like to use in your life?

   _____

   _____

LIFESKILLS ▶ My schedule is crazy

Before You Watch

A. Look at the picture and answer the questions.

1. What's wrong with Hector?
2. What do you think Naomi is saying to Hector?

While You Watch

B. ▶ Watch the video and complete the dialog.

Naomi: . . . you wouldn't skip a day of work, either. Treat your studies in the same way, and your grades will (1) _____improve_____.

Hector: That's a great (2) _____, thanks.

Naomi: Well, now you know what you have to do. So go do it! If you get (3) _____, you'll feel more productive. Trust me!

Hector: (4) _____ give it a try. What have I got to lose, right?

Naomi: Good luck. Tell me how it's (5) _____ later on.

Hector: I (6) _____. Talk to you later.

Check Your Understanding

C. Circle the correct word to complete each sentence.

1. There's too much noise and it's difficult for Hector to (communicate/concentrate).

2. Hector says his (schedule/organization) is crazy and he has no time to study.

3. Naomi suggests that Hector (make time/write down) where and when he's going to study.

4. A schedule will help Hector to (get organized/spend time with friends).

5. Naomi tells Hector a schedule will make him (productive/smarter).

Review

A. Exchange books with a partner. Have your partner complete the schedule.

	Monday	Tuesday	Wednesday	Thursday	Friday	Saturday	Sunday
MORNING							
AFTERNOON							
EVENING							

B. Write sentences about your partner's schedule using the frequency adverbs.

1. (always) _____

2. (usually) _____

3. (often) _____

4. (sometimes) _____

5. (rarely) _____

6. (never) _____

C. Now share your sentences with your partner and see if he or she agrees. Use the conversation below as a model.

Student A: You always work in the evenings.
Student B: Yes, I do.

D. Complete the sentences with the correct verb form.

1. When Jason _____ (get) a better job, he _____ (buy) a new house.

2. Lilia _____ (join) her sister at college when she _____ (finish) her ESL class.

3. We _____ (run) a marathon when we _____ (complete) our training program.

4. When Maria _____ (get) her bachelor's degree, she _____ (ask) her boss for a raise.

E. **What are your goals for the future? Write sentences about your future goals using *when*.**

1. *When I finish this course, I will take the GED exam.*

2. _____

3. _____

4. _____

5. _____

F. **Think of one obstacle and one solution for each goal you wrote in Exercise E. Complete the chart.**

	Goal	Obstacle	Solution
1.			
2.			
3.			
4.			

G. **Match each word or phrase to its correct meaning. Draw a line.**

1. paragraph

2. topic sentence

3. support sentences

4. conclusion sentence

a. introduces your topic, or main idea

b. give details about your topic

c. gives a summary of everything you wrote

d. a group of sentences about the same topic

Learner Log

I can analyze study habits.　　　I can manage time.
■ Yes　■ No　■ Maybe　　　　■ Yes　■ No　■ Maybe

H. Read the following sentences that make up a paragraph. Label each as a *topic* sentence (T), a *support* sentence (S), or a *conclusion* sentence (C). Remember, there can only be one topic sentence and one conclusion sentence.

1. I will buy books to study with and I will study very hard. _____

2. Within the next two years, I hope to have my license. _____

3. When I'm ready, I will register for the test. _____

4. My goal for the future is to get my real estate license. _____

5. When I am close to taking the test, I will ask my friend to help me. _____

I. On a separate piece of paper, rewrite the sentences above in the correct order using correct paragraph formatting.

J. Write two good study habits.

1. _____

2. _____

K. Write two good time-management strategies.

1. _____

2. _____

L. Write the correct word or phrase from the box for each definition.

beneficial	concentrate	distractions	go over
goal	harmful	improve	obstacle

1. bad for you　　　　　　　　　　　　_____

2. when you get better at something　　_____

3. good for you　　　　　　　　　　　_____

4. think hard about something　　　　　_____

5. something you want to achieve　　　_____

6. a problem　　　　　　　　　　　　_____

7. review something or check it again　_____

8. things that bother you when you are studying _____

TEAM PROJECT ✔ Make a schedule

With a team, you will design a weekly schedule that includes your class and study time. You will identify good study habits and time-management strategies.

1. **COLLABORATE** Form a team with four or five students. Choose a position for each member of your team.

Position	Job description	Student name
Student 1: Leader	Check that everyone speaks English and participates.	
Student 2: Secretary	Take notes on study habits and time-management strategies.	
Student 3: Designer	Design a weekly schedule.	
Students 4/5: Assistants	Help the secretary and the designer with their work.	

2. Design a weekly schedule. On your schedule, write in the days and times you have English class.

3. Decide on a goal that is related to learning English. Then, think of one obstacle to your goal and two solutions.

4. Make a list of good study habits and a list of time-management strategies you would like to use.

5. Make a poster with all of the information from above: weekly schedule, goal, obstacle, solutions, good study habits, and time-management strategies.

6. Present your poster to the class.

Public libraries, such as the New York Public Library, often have resources like free English conversation groups once a week to support the local community.

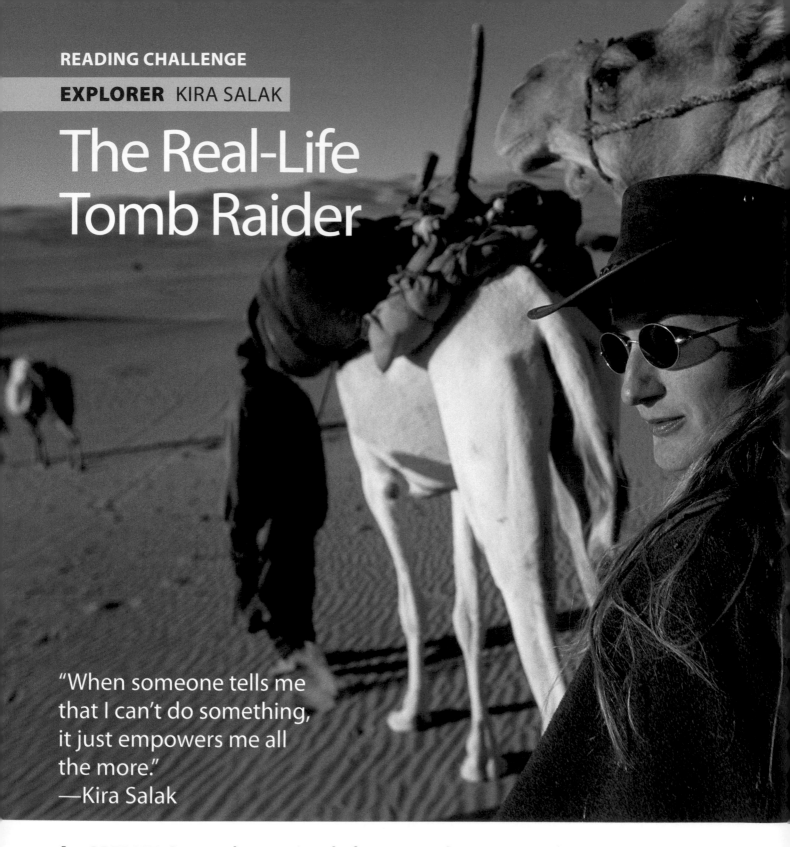

EXPLORER KIRA SALAK

The Real-Life Tomb Raider

"When someone tells me that I can't do something, it just empowers me all the more."
—Kira Salak

A. PREDICT Answer the questions before you read.

1. Read the title. What do you think the article will be about?

2. Look at the picture and read the quote. Do you think Kira has goals? Why?

3. Look at the picture again. Where do you think Kira is?

B. **What do you think these words mean? Work with a partner.**

adventurer	continent	document (v)	doubt
empower	escape	exotic	kayak (v)
kidnap	resolve	superficial	terrifying

C. **Read about Kira Salak.**

Kira Salak is an adventurer. She was the first known person to kayak down the Niger River in West Africa by herself. Kira is a traveler. She has traveled alone to almost every continent. Kira is a writer. She documents her travels by writing about the people she has met and the places she has seen. How did she become all of these things?

Kira wrote her first short story at the age of six. Her imagination always took her to wild and exotic places. At age 19, she took her first solo trip, hoping to have new and unique experiences. At age 20, while backpacking through Africa, she was kidnapped by soldiers and forced to "make a terrifying escape." But this experience didn't stop her. In fact, since then, she has purposely traveled to more dangerous countries so she can tell the world about the people who live there.

Kira's experiences empower her. Even though she has seen some terrible things, she is still hopeful. Her goal is to find common ground with other people. "When you get beyond politics and superficial cultural differences, people all want the same things: peace, happiness, success for their children, and the best standard of life." Kira is a writer, a traveler, and an adventurer. But above all else, she is a human being. "When someone tells me I can't do something, it just empowers me all the more. People's doubts in my ability only strengthen my resolve. When they say I can't accomplish a challenge, I just eat that up."

D. **SUPPORT** Underline the answers to the questions below in the reading. Write the question number next to the evidence.

1. How do we know that Kira wanted to travel from a young age?

2. When did she first travel alone?

3. What empowers Kira?

4. Where was she kidnapped?

E. **SUMMARIZE** Without looking at the reading, tell your partner about Kira's goal, an obstacle, and a solution.

Consumer Smarts

A woman shops for a dress
at a fashion store.

UNIT OUTCOMES

- [ ] Identify places to purchase goods and services
- [ ] Interpret advertisements
- [ ] Compare products
- [ ] Identify and compare purchasing methods
- [ ] Make a smart purchase

Look at the photo and answer the questions.

1. Where are the women?
2. What goods can be purchased in this place?

Shopping for goods and services

GOAL ■ Identify places to purchase goods and services

A. **Look at the pictures. What goods or services can you purchase at these places?**

B. **CLASSIFY** **Which of the places below sell goods and which sell services? Which sell both? Complete the diagram.**

~~laundromat~~	gas station	dry cleaners	tailor
jewelry store	bank	pharmacy	department store
~~grocery store~~	car wash	~~post office~~	hair salon

Sell goods | **Sell services**

grocery store   post office   laundromat

C. EXPLAIN Where can you purchase each of the following items? Write the places. Some items may have more than one answer.

1. medicine   _____pharmacy_____

2. a table   _____

3. a notebook   _____

4. a bracelet   _____

5. boots   _____

6. a refrigerator   _____

7. bread   _____

8. motor oil   _____

9. a shirt   _____

10. stamps   _____

D. We use the expression *to get something done* when we talk about services we purchase. Study the chart with your teacher.

To Get Something Done				
Subject	*get*	**Object**	**Past participle**	**Example sentence**
I	get	my hair	cut	I get my hair cut every month. (present)
She	got	her clothes	cleaned	She got her clothes cleaned yesterday. (past)
For a list of past participles, see pages 214–219.				

He gets his suits made at the tailor.

E. **Where can you receive the following services? Some items may have more than one answer.**

1. get your hair cut   *hair salon*

2. get your checks cashed   _____

3. get your clothes repaired   _____

4. get your car washed   _____

5. get your car fixed   _____

6. get your clothes washed   _____

F. **Answer the following questions with complete sentences.**

1. Where do you get your hair cut?

   I get my hair cut at the hair salon. _____

2. Where did you get your prescription filled?

   _____

3. Where do you get your packages mailed?

   _____

4. Where did you get your keys made?

   _____

5. Where did you get your gas tank filled up?

   _____

6. Where do you get your clothes washed?

   _____

G. **APPLY** **Imagine you are new to the neighborhood. Ask your partner questions about places in the area.**

EXAMPLE: **Student A:** Where can I get my car washed?

                  Student B: At the car wash on Maple Street.

H. **Next time you go to the mall, look at the directory. What different stores and businesses does it have? Make a list to share with your class.**

LESSON ② Advertisements

GOAL ■ Interpret advertisements

A. FIND OUT Discuss the following questions with your classmates.

1. What are advertisements? Where can you find them?

2. What information can you find in advertisements?

B. Read the advertisements.

1.

SAVE ON AN OIL CHANGE AT BOB'S AUTO SERVICE

Most cars now only $29.95.
Includes up to five quarts of oil,
new oil filter, and labor.

Offer expires August 5th
CLICK HERE FOR AN ESTIMATE

2.

FUN FOR THE ENTIRE FAMILY WITH THE NEW ENERX SYSTEM

Watch movies and live TV, listen
to music, AND play games with
this all-in-one system.

Register now for free installation
CLICK HERE

3.

STEREO FACTORY OUTLET SALE
CLICK HERE

Stereo speakers starting at $79.95
a pair and headphones
starting at $9.95 a pair.

30%-70% off original prices
$5 discount with code: STEREO5

4.

BIKE SALE AT WHEEL WORLD

SAVE 25%
Regular-priced bikes at $150 now
on sale for $112.50.
All bikes come with a one-year
warranty.

CLICK HERE TO VISIT OUR SITE

C. INTERPRET Read the ads and find words with these meanings.

1. discount ___*on sale*___

2. guarantee _____

3. work _____

4. to come to an end _____

5. no charge _____

6. approximate cost _____

7. to set up for use _____

8. normal _____

D. Read the ads again and choose the correct answers.

1. What does the oil change NOT include?
   - ☐ oil
   - ☐ oil filter
   - ☐ windshield wiper fluid

2. When does the offer expire for the oil change?
   - ☐ May 8th
   - ☐ August 8th
   - ☐ August 5th

3. What does the entertainment system not include?
   - ☐ live TV
   - ☐ music
   - ☐ speakers

4. How much is the entertainment system?
   - ☐ $150
   - ☐ $79.95
   - ☐ It doesn't say.

5. According to the ad, who is the entertainment system good for?
   - ☐ dads
   - ☐ kids
   - ☐ the entire family

6. What is for sale at the stereo factory outlet?
   - ☐ stereo speakers
   - ☐ headphones
   - ☐ stereo speakers and headphones

7. What is the discount at the stereo factory outlet?
   - ☐ $9.95
   - ☐ 30–70%
   - ☐ $79.95

8. What is the regular price of the bikes?
   - ☐ $150.00
   - ☐ $112.99
   - ☐ $250.00

9. How much are the bikes discounted?
   - ☐ $25
   - ☐ 25%
   - ☐ $37.00

10. Which item(s) come with a warranty?
    - ☐ entertainment systems
    - ☐ bicycles
    - ☐ entertainment systems and bicycles

E. EVALUATE Which product do you like the best? Why?

_____

_____

_____

F. Read the two ads and complete the table.

Cleaning Services		
Company	Happy Helpers	Kate's Cleaners
Phone Number		
Product or Service		
Price		
Discounts		
Other Information		

G. JUSTIFY Which cleaning service would you choose? Why?

_____

_____

H. Choose a product or service you want to sell. On a separate piece of paper, create the same table as the one in Exercise F and complete it.

I. APPLY Find some newspaper advertisements or print out some ads from the Internet. What special offers can you find?

GOAL ■ Compare products

A. IDENTIFY Label the different parts of the laptop. Write the numbers.

1. headphone jack	2. power cable jack	3. power cable	4. touch pad
5. keyboard	6. screen	7. CD drive	8. USB port

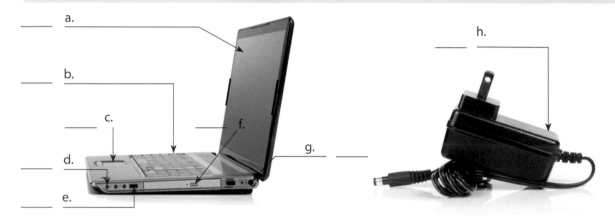

B. What should you look for when you buy a laptop? Point to the adjectives.

Speed: Is the computer *fast* or *slow*? **Price:** Is the computer *expensive* or *cheap*?

Screen: Is the screen *narrow* or *wide*? **Hard Drive:** Is the hard drive *big* or *small*?

Memory: How much memory does the computer have?

Speed	Memory and hard drive	Screen size
GHz = gigahertz 1,000 MHz = 1 GHz	MB = megabytes 1,000 MB = 1 GB GB = gigabytes TB = terabytes	15" = 15 inches

C. DESCRIBE Use the adjectives from Exercise B to talk about the laptops in the table.

EXAMPLE: The JCN laptop has a wide screen.

	JCN	Doshiba	Vintel	Shepland	Kontaq
Price	$1,999	$2,499	$1,499	$1,799	$1,299
Screen size	15"	15"	17"	13"	13"
Speed	2.6GHz	2.6GHz	2.5GHz	2.8GHz	2.2GHz
Memory	8GB	16GB	4GB	8GB	4GB
Hard drive	512GB	1TB	256GB	512GB	256GB

D. **Study the chart with your classmates and teacher.**

Comparatives				
	Adjective	**Comparative**	**Rule**	**Example sentence**
Short adjectives	cheap	cheap**er**	Add *-er* to the end of the adjective.	Your computer was *cheaper* than my computer.
Long adjectives	expensive	**more** expensive	Add *more* before the adjective.	The new computer was *more expensive* than the old one.
Irregular adjectives	good, bad	better, worse	These adjectives are irregular.	The computer at school is *better* than this one.

*Remember to use *than* after a comparative adjective followed by a noun.

E. **Use the rules in Exercise D and the spelling rules to make comparative adjectives.**

1. slow   _____slower_____   2. small   _____

3. wide   _____   4. big   _____

5. heavy   _____   6. fast   _____

7. beautiful _____   8. interesting _____

SPELLING RULES		
hot	→	**hotter**
easy	→	**easier**
large	→	**larger**
pretty	→	**prettier**

F. **Make comparative sentences about the laptops in Exercise C.**

1. The Kontaq / slow / the Vintel

   The Kontaq is slower than the Vintel. _____

2. The JCN screen / wide / the Shepland screen

_____

3. The Doshiba / fast / the Vintel

_____

4. The JCN's hard drive / big / the Kontaq's

_____

G. **EVALUATE** **Talk to your partner. Which laptop from Exercise C would you buy? Using comparatives, give three reasons for your choice.**

H. Study the chart with your teacher.

Superlatives				
	Adjective	**Superlative**	**Rule**	**Example sentence**
Short adjectives	cheap	**the** cheap**est**	Add *the* before and *-est* to the end of the adjective.	Your computer is *the cheapest*.
Long adjectives	expensive	**the most** expensive	Add *the most* before the adjective.	He bought *the most* expensive computer in the store.
Irregular adjectives	good, bad	the best, the worst	These adjectives are irregular.	The computers at school are *the best*.
*Always use *the* before a superlative.				

I. Use the rules in Exercise H and the spelling rules to make superlative adjectives.

1. slow ___the slowest___   2. small _____

3. wide _____   4. big _____

5. heavy _____   6. fast _____

7. beautiful _____   8. interesting _____

SPELLING RULES		
hot	→	**the hottest**
easy	→	**the easiest**
large	→	**the largest**
pretty	→	**the prettiest**

J. Make superlative sentences about the laptops in Exercise C.

1. wide ___The Vintel laptop has the widest screen._____

2. expensive _____

3. cheap _____

4. slow _____

5. large memory _____

6. small memory _____

K. **APPLY** Write six questions about the laptops in Exercise C using comparatives and superlatives. Ask your classmates to answer your questions.

EXAMPLE: Which laptop is faster, the JCN or the Vintel?

LESSON 4 Cash or charge?

GOAL ▪ Identify and compare purchasing methods

A. IDENTIFY Terron uses four different ways to make purchases. What are they?

B. Write the correct word next to its description. You will use some of the items twice.

cash	personal check	credit card	debit card

1. This is a written request to your bank asking them to pay money out of your account.

   _____

2. This allows you to borrow money to make purchases. _____

3. Coins and bills are this. _____

4. This allows a store to take money directly from your account to pay for purchases.

   _____

5. This allows you to buy now and pay later. _____

6. You can get cash out of the ATM with this. _____

C. **COMPARE** Talk about the advantages and disadvantages of each purchasing method. Use the conversation below as a model. Then, complete the table.

Student A: Cash is good because it is quick and easy.

Student B: Yes, but if you lose cash, you cannot replace it.

	Cash	Debit card	Personal check	Credit card
Advantages	quick and easy			
Disadvantages	can't replace			

D. Talk to a partner about the purchasing method you prefer and why.

E. Listen to Terron and his wife, Leilani, talk about purchasing methods. Make a list of the things they *have to* do and *must* do.

Have to	*Must*

F. We use *must* and *have to* when something is necessary. *Must* is a little stronger than *have to*. Study the chart below with your teacher.

Must vs. Have to			
Subject	**Modal**	**Base verb**	**Example sentence**
I, He, She, It, You, We, They	have to must	save pay off	I have to save money for a vacation. I must pay off my credit card every month.

G. Complete each statement with *must* or *have to* and a verb from the box.

check	keep	put	make	pay

1. You ____must____ ____pay____ your bills if you want a good credit history.

2. You _____ _____ your cash in a safe place.

3. You _____ _____ track of the personal checks you write.

4. You _____ _____ the minimum amount on your credit card every month.

5. You _____ _____ sure you have enough money in the bank when you write a personal check.

6. You _____ _____ your balance before you get cash out of an ATM.

H. **APPLY** Choose one purchasing method and write a paragraph on why you think it is better than the rest. Use comparative and superlative adjectives.

_____

_____

_____

_____

_____

_____

_____

_____

_____

LESSON ⑤ Think before you buy

GOAL ■ Make a smart purchase

A. Read about making smart purchases.

> You make a smart purchase when you think and plan before you buy something. First of all, you make a decision to buy something. This is the easy part. The second step is comparison shopping. You comparison shop by reading advertisements, going to different stores, and talking to friends and family. Third, you choose which product you are going to buy.
>
> Do you have enough money to buy this product? If you don't, the next step is to start saving. This may take a while depending on how much you need to save. Once you have enough money, you are ready to make your purchase. If you follow these steps to make a purchase, you will be a smart consumer. And smart consumers make smart purchases!

B. PUT IN ORDER Order the steps from 1 to 5 according to the passage above.

_____ make the purchase   _____ read advertisements

___1___ decide to buy something   _____ choose the best deal

_____ save money

C. Rewrite the steps in Exercise B after the words below.

First, _decide to buy something_____.

Second, _____.

Next, _____.

Then, _____.

Finally, _____.

Save more money by comparison shopping on everyday items.

D. *Sequencing transitions* are used to describe stages of a process. Study the examples in the box.

First,	First of all,	Second,	Second of all,	Third,
Fourth,	Next,	Then,	Lastly,	Finally,

E. **Put the steps in the correct order.**

> **YOU**
> Use *you* to talk about people in general.

_____ You decide to buy it.

_____ You find out the price.

__1__ You see something in a store you want to buy.

_____ You decide to use your credit card.

_____ You think about if you have enough money to pay for it or not.

_____ You pay for it.

_____ You think about if you want to pay cash or use your credit card.

F. **Add sequencing transitions to the steps above to write a paragraph about making a smart purchase.**

_____

_____

_____

_____

_____

_____

_____

_____

_____

_____

_____

G. APPLY Imagine you are going to buy a laptop. In groups, come up with a list of steps to make a smart purchase.

1. _____
2. _____
3. _____
4. _____
5. _____
6. _____
7. _____
8. _____

H. COMPOSE Write a paragraph about buying a laptop. Use sequencing transitions.

_____
_____
_____
_____
_____
_____
_____
_____
_____
_____
_____
_____

Before You Watch

A. Look at the picture and answer the questions.

1. Where are Mr. and Mrs. Sanchez?

2. What is the couple looking at? Why?

While You Watch

B. Watch the video and complete the dialog.

Mr. Sanchez: Compare the laptop to a (1) _____ *desktop* _____ computer.

Mrs. Sanchez: The desktop computer is a lot bigger and heavier than the (2) _____.

Mr. Sanchez: Yes, but it's (3) _____.

Mrs. Sanchez: Let's see. The laptop is smaller than the desktop, but it's also (4) _____ than the desktop.

Mr. Sanchez: Right.

Mrs. Sanchez: Which one has the (5) _____ memory?

Check Your Understanding

C. Show the correct order of events by writing a number next to each sentence.

a. _____ Mr. Sanchez says the laptop is on sale today.

b. _____ Hector comes home carrying Mateo's old laptop.

c. _____ Mr. and Mrs. Sanchez compare laptops and desktops.

d. _____ Mr. Sanchez says Hector needs a computer for school.

e. _____ Mr. and Mrs. Sanchez agree to surprise Hector with a new laptop.

Review

A. Where can you purchase the following goods or services? Write the places below.

1. shampoo _____

2. soccer ball _____

3. stamps _____

4. prescription refill _____

5. a washing machine _____

6. fruit _____

7. clothes cleaned _____

8. shoes _____

B. Write the present tense form of *get* and the past participle of the verb in parentheses.

1. He _____gets_____ his car _____washed_____ at the local car wash. (wash)

2. She _____ her hair _____ at the hair salon. (cut)

3. He _____ his car _____ at the automotive shop. (fix)

4. They _____ their clothes _____ at the dry cleaners. (clean)

C. Read the ads and answer the questions below.

Hill's Xonda
Xonda Pilot with all the bells and whistles
$36,999
Includes free gas for a year!

Xonda of Albilene
Fully loaded Xonda Pilot
$37,999
(includes tax, title, and license)
Come test drive your new car!
0% financing

1. Which car is cheaper? _____

2. What is good about the offer from Hill's? _____

3. What is good about the offer from Albilene? _____

4. Which dealership would you buy from? _____

   Why? _____

D. Complete the following statements with a comparative or a superlative adjective. Use *than* where necessary.

1. My new watch was _____*cheaper than*_____ my old watch. (cheap)

2. This computer is _____ one in the store. (fast)

3. That mirror is _____ the one we have now. (tall)

4. This box is much _____ that one. What's in it? (heavy)

5. _____ paintings in the world are painted by that artist. (beautiful)

6. Do you think that the book is _____ the movie? (interesting)

7. I always pay by credit card. It's _____ way to pay. (easy)

8. My neighbor's house is _____ our house. (big)

9. Do you think this car is _____ the one you have? (good)

E. Imagine that you are going to buy a new car—your dream car. Write sentences comparing your old car to your new car.

My new car is faster than my old car.

_____

_____

_____

F. What is the best restaurant in your neighborhood? Write sentences comparing this restaurant to all the other restaurants in the neighborhood.

China Palace has the friendliest service in the neighborhood.

_____

_____

_____

_____

Learner Log

I can identify and compare purchasing methods.   I can make a smart purchase.

■ Yes   ■ No   ■ Maybe   ■ Yes   ■ No   ■ Maybe

G. Write a sentence about each of the following purchasing methods. Use *must* or *have to*.

1. cashier's check: _You must be careful not to lose a cashier's check._____

2. cash: _____

3. personal check: _____

4. debit card: _____

5. credit card: _____

H. Imagine that your friend is going to buy a new television. What steps would you tell him or her to take? Write them below.

1. _____

2. _____

3. _____

4. _____

5. _____

I. Write a paragraph using the steps you wrote above. Use sequencing transitions.

_____

_____

_____

_____

J. Choose four words from this unit. Write each word and an example sentence on an index card. Study the words while you are traveling to school or eating your breakfast.

to purchase	
	_____ the shirt

Two advertisements and a purchase plan

1. **COLLABORATE** Form a team with four or five students. Choose positions for each member of your team.

Position	Job description	Student name
Student 1: Team Leader	Check that everyone speaks English. Check that everyone participates.	
Student 2: Secretary	Write the advertisement. Take notes for the family team.	
Student 3: Designer	Design an advertisement layout.	
Students 4/5: Spokespeople	Plan presentations.	

Part 1—Advertising Team: Create Advertisements

1. Create two different advertisements for the same product or service.

2. Present your ads to the class and then post them in the classroom.

Part 2—Family: Create a Purchase Plan

1. Walk around the room and choose a product or service to buy from all the ads on the wall.

2. Compare two of the ads, writing four comparative statements about why one is better than the other.

3. Choose one product or service to buy and write a purchase plan—the steps needed to make a smart purchase.

4. Present your comparisons and purchase plan to the class.

EXPLORER TRISTRAM STUART

Customer Responsibility

"Eat what you buy, buy
what you need, and use
your power as customer
and citizen to demand
that the businesses you
buy from also stop wasting
food." —Tristram Stuart

A. PREDICT Answer the questions below in a small group.

1. Read the quote. What does it mean?

2. Do you think businesses waste food? How?

3. What could you do to stop wasting food?

B. Scan the article for the underlined words and phrases. What do they mean? Work
with a partner.

C. Read about Tristram Stuart.

(1) When Tristram Stuart was 15 years old, he bought some pigs. He fed the pigs <u>leftover food</u> from the school cafeteria and other local businesses. That's when he saw how much food is wasted every day. Growing up as an <u>environmentalist</u>, he learned that rainforests were being cut down to grow more food. There were also millions of hungry people in the world. Tristram believes that we already grow enough food to feed nine billion people, so we have to use it more carefully and waste less.

(2) Tristram is now an author and <u>activist</u> fighting a war against <u>food-waste</u>. One-third of the world's food is wasted from the time it is grown to the time it gets to your plate. One reason is because businesses want the most attractive food to sell to their customers. There are over one billion hungry people who could be fed on less than a quarter of the food wasted in the United States and Europe.

(3) Tristram set up the charity Feedback, which has started three programs to let the world know about the food-waste problem and to help come up with <u>solutions</u>. One of his programs is called Feeding the 5000. This is a free <u>public feast</u> of food that would have been wasted. The focus of his Pig Idea campaign is to convince the government to allow feeding waste to pigs again. He also started the Gleaning Network, which sends volunteers into fields to pick the leftover produce that would otherwise go bad. The food is then given to groups that give to the hungry.

(4) Tristram's mission is to get everyone to "eat what you buy, buy what you need, and use your power as customer and citizen to demand that the businesses you buy from also stop wasting food."

D. ANALYZE Write the paragraph number where each piece of information can be found.

Information	Paragraph
Tristram started Feeding the 5000.	
Tristram first saw that food was being wasted.	
His mission is to get everyone to stop wasting food.	
He is fighting a war against food waste.	

E. SUMMARIZE On a separate piece of paper, summarize the three programs Tristram started.

Would you eat
these strawberries?

Housing

In cities where there is little space, tall apartment buildings are the only way to accommodate people.

UNIT OUTCOMES

- [ ] Interpret classified ads
- [ ] Make decisions
- [ ] Arrange and cancel utilities
- [ ] Create a budget
- [ ] Write a formal letter

Look at the photo and answer the questions.

1. What type of housing do you see?

2. How many bedrooms do you think this type of housing has? What else does it have?

LESSON ① House hunting

GOAL ■ Interpret classified ads

A. **EXPLAIN** Think about the place where you live. How did you find it? What are some different ways to find housing?

B. One way to find housing is through classified ads online. Write the titles of the following ads and rank them in order from your favorite (1) to least favorite (6).

Sunny studio	Spacious four-bedroom
Sunny one-bedroom with high ceilings	Large apartment with garage and pool
~~Two-bedroom in a gated community~~	Charming condo with balcony

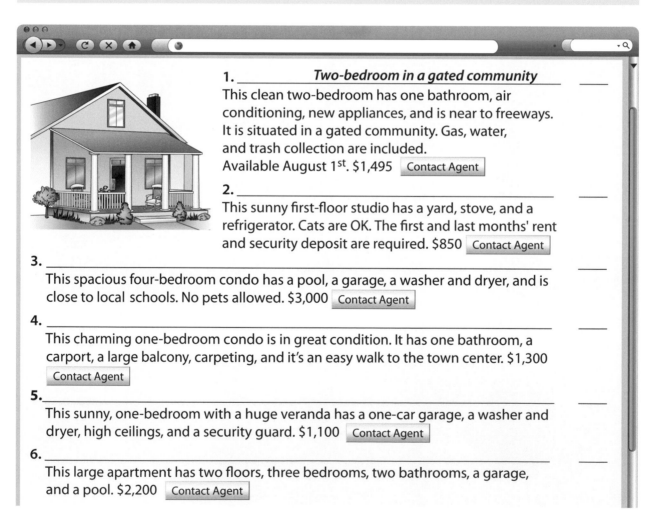

1. _____ *Two-bedroom in a gated community* ____
This clean two-bedroom has one bathroom, air conditioning, new appliances, and is near to freeways. It is situated in a gated community. Gas, water, and trash collection are included.
Available August 1st. $1,495 [Contact Agent]

2. _____ ____
This sunny first-floor studio has a yard, stove, and a refrigerator. Cats are OK. The first and last months' rent and security deposit are required. $850 [Contact Agent]

3. _____ ____
This spacious four-bedroom condo has a pool, a garage, a washer and dryer, and is close to local schools. No pets allowed. $3,000 [Contact Agent]

4. _____ ____
This charming one-bedroom condo is in great condition. It has one bathroom, a carport, a large balcony, carpeting, and it's an easy walk to the town center. $1,300 [Contact Agent]

5. _____ ____
This sunny, one-bedroom with a huge veranda has a one-car garage, a washer and dryer, high ceilings, and a security guard. $1,100 [Contact Agent]

6. _____ ____
This large apartment has two floors, three bedrooms, two bathrooms, a garage, and a pool. $2,200 [Contact Agent]

C. Work with a partner and make a list of the housing vocabulary in Exercise B that is new to you. Discuss with your classmates and teacher.

D. **COMPARE** Discuss the following questions about the ads in Exercise B with your partner.

1. Which one-bedroom apartment has higher rent?

2. Look at ads 1 and 5. Which apartment has more bedrooms?

3. Look at ads 1 and 6. Which apartment has more bathrooms?

E. **Study the charts.**

Comparatives Using Nouns	
Our new apartment has *more bedrooms* than our old one. Our old apartment had *fewer bedrooms* than our new one.	Use *more* or *fewer* to compare count nouns.
Rachel's apartment gets *more light* than Pablo's apartment. Pablo's apartment gets *less light* than Rachel's apartment.	Use *more* or *less* to compare noncount nouns.

Superlatives Using Nouns	
Rachel's apartment has *the most bedrooms*. Phuong's apartment has *the fewest bedrooms*.	Use *the most* or *the fewest* for count nouns.
Rachel's apartment has *the most light*. Phuong's apartment has *the least light*.	Use *the most* or *the least* for noncount nouns.

F. **Complete the sentences with *more* or *most*.**

1. Kim's house has _____ bedrooms than Jen's house.

2. The Worshams' apartment gets the _____ light.

3. That condo has _____ appliances than this one.

4. Her house has the _____ rooms.

G. **Complete the sentences with *fewer, less, fewest,* or *least*.**

1. John's house has _____ bathrooms than Brad's place.

2. The small condo has _____ light than the big one.

3. The small condo has the _____ space.

4. Their apartment has the _____ windows.

H. **SCAN** Work with a partner. Scan the rental ads and ask and answer the questions. Try to answer in complete sentences.

a. This first-floor apartment has two bedrooms, 1.5 bathrooms, a garage, and a gym.
Price: $1275 per month **Security deposit:** $500 Contact Agent

b. This large five-bedroom, two-bathroom house with a two-car garage, washer/dryer hookups, and high ceilings is in a quiet neighborhood.
Price: $3200 per month **Security deposit:** $2000 Contact Agent

c. This beautiful three-bedroom condo has three bathrooms, a garage for two cars, a large patio, and wood floors. It is located close to local shops.
Price: $1700 per month **Security deposit:** $600 Contact Agent

d. This bright top-floor studio has a balcony and new appliances. Cats are OK. First and last months' rent are due at signing.
Price: $1000 per month **Security deposit:** $550 Contact Agent

1. Which place has more bathrooms: the house or the condo?

2. Which place has the most bedrooms?

3. Which place has the highest rent?

4. Which place has more bedrooms: the condo or the apartment?

5. Which place has the lowest security deposit?

SCAN
Quickly look for the answers in a text without reading everything.

I. Write sentences using comparatives and superlatives to compare the rentals in Exercise H.

1. _The apartment has fewer bedrooms than the house._____.

2. _____

3. _____

4. _____

5. _____

6. _____

J. Search for classified housing ads on the Internet. Find an ad that you like and write it down to share with the class.

GOAL ■ Make decisions

A. Read about the Nguyen family.

The Nguyen family lives in Cedarville, Texas. Vu Nguyen came from Vietnam twenty years ago and met his wife, Maryanne, in Texas. The Nguyens have four children—two sons and two daughters. They are currently living in a two-bedroom apartment, which is too small for all six of them. They would like to stay in Cedarville, but they need a bigger place. Vu recently got a raise at work, so the Nguyen family wants to move.

🎧
CD 1
TR 7
B. INTERPRET Listen to the Nguyen family talk about their housing preferences. Check the boxes next to the things they would like to have in their new apartment.

☐ 2 bedrooms	☐ tennis courts	☐ yard
☐ 3 bedrooms	☐ pool	☐ air-conditioning
☐ 2 bathrooms	☐ security guard	☐ carpeting
☐ 3 bathrooms	☐ big windows	☐ balcony
☐ convenient location	☐ garage	☐ washer/dryer

C. Compare your answers with a partner.

D. **Study the chart with your classmates and teacher.**

Yes/No Questions and Answers with *Do*				
Questions				**Short answers**
Do	**Subject**	**Base verb**	**Example question**	
Do	I, you, we, they	have	Do they have a yard?	Yes, they do. / No, they don't.
Does	he, she, it	want	Does she want air conditioning?	Yes, she does. / No, she doesn't.

E. **Practice asking and answering *yes/no* questions with a partner. Use the Nguyen family preferences in Exercise B.**

Student A: Do they want <u>five bedrooms</u>?
Student B: No, they don't.

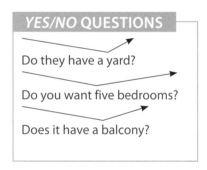

YES/NO QUESTIONS

Do they have a yard?

Do you want five bedrooms?

Does it have a balcony?

F. **CONSTRUCT** **Write *yes/no* questions you could ask the Nguyens.**

1. _Do you want a bathtub?_____

2. _____

3. _____

4. _____

5. _____

6. _____

G. **With a partner, practice asking your questions.**

H. VISUALIZE Imagine you are going to buy or rent a new home. Write the number of bedrooms and bathrooms you prefer. Then, check your preferences. Add other preferences that are not on the list.

_____ bedrooms

☐ convenient location

_____ bathrooms

☐ garage

☐ yard

☐ carport

☐ balcony

☐ refrigerator

☐ pool

☐ _____

☐ washer/dryer

☐ _____

☐ air conditioning

☐ _____

I. Write five _yes/no_ questions you can ask your partner about his or her housing preferences. Don't write the answers yet.

1. _Do you want a balcony?_ _____

Answer: _____

2. _____

Answer: _____

3. _____

Answer: _____

4. _____

Answer: _____

5. _____

Answer: _____

6. _____

Answer: _____

J. Practice asking your questions with a partner. Fill in the answers in Exercise I.

LESSON ③ Paying the bills

GOAL ▪ Arrange and cancel utilities

A. Discuss these questions with your classmates.

1. What are utilities?

2. What utilities do you pay for?

3. If you rent, does your landlord pay for any utilities?

4. What information can you find on your utility bills?

<table>
<tr><td colspan="2">INFORMATION QUESTIONS</td></tr>
<tr><td>What's your address?</td></tr>
<tr><td>Where do you live?</td></tr>
<tr><td>When will you be moving?</td></tr>
</table>

B. INTERPRET Read the gas bill and answer the questions.

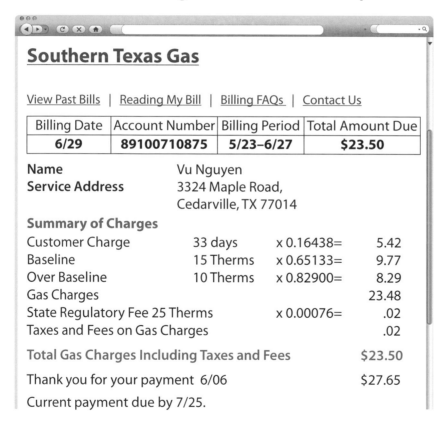

Southern Texas Gas

View Past Bills | Reading My Bill | Billing FAQs | Contact Us

Billing Date	Account Number	Billing Period	Total Amount Due
6/29	89100710875	5/23–6/27	$23.50

Name Vu Nguyen
Service Address 3324 Maple Road,
Cedarville, TX 77014

Summary of Charges

Customer Charge	33 days	x 0.16438=	5.42
Baseline	15 Therms	x 0.65133=	9.77
Over Baseline	10 Therms	x 0.82900=	8.29
Gas Charges			23.48
State Regulatory Fee 25 Therms		x 0.00076=	.02
Taxes and Fees on Gas Charges			.02

Total Gas Charges Including Taxes and Fees $23.50

Thank you for your payment 6/06 $27.65

Current payment due by 7/25.

1. What is Vu's account number? _____

2. How much is their gas bill this month? _____

3. How much did they pay last month? _____

4. Which bill was more expensive: this month's or last month's? _____

5. When is the latest the payment can be made? _____

C. Vu and his family are getting ready to move. Vu calls the electric company to speak to a customer service representative. Listen and write short answers for the following information.

1. Name of the company: _____

2. Name of the representative: _____

3. When Vu wants service turned off: _____

4. When Vu wants service turned on: _____

D. **INTERPRET** Listen to the recording again and answer the questions.

1. The first voice is recorded and gives four choices. What are they?

   a. *get new service or cancel existing service* _____

   b. _____

   c. _____

   d. _____

2. What information does Vu give to the gas company?

   a. *his current address* _____

   b. _____

   c. _____

   d. _____

People are investing in alternative sources of power. This house has solar panels on the roof to help generate electricity.

E. Study the chart.

Information Questions	
Question words	**Example questions**
How	*How* may I help you?
What	*What* is your current address?
When	*When* would you like your service turned off?

F. Listen to the conversation and read. As you listen, underline the information questions.

CD 1
TR 9

Recording:	Thank you for calling Southern Texas Gas. Your call is very important to us. Please wait for the next available customer service representative.
Representative:	Hello, my name is Liam. How may I help you?
Vu:	Um, yes. My family is moving next week, and we need to have our gas turned off here and get the gas turned on in our new home.
Representative:	What is your current address?
Vu:	3324 Maple Road.
Representative:	What is your name, sir?
Vu:	Vu Nguyen.
Representative:	When would you like the gas turned off?
Vu:	Next Wednesday, please.
Representative:	And what is your new address?
Vu:	5829 Bay Road.
Representative:	And when would you like the gas turned on in your new home?
Vu:	This Monday, please.
Representative:	OK. Your current service will be turned off sometime between seven and nine o'clock on Wednesday the 11th, and your new service will be on before eight on Monday morning, the 9th. Is there anything else I can do for you?
Vu:	No, that's it.
Representative:	Thank you for calling Southern Texas Gas. Have a nice day.
Vu:	Thanks. You, too.

G. Practice the conversation in Exercise F. Make a new conversation using your own information. Remember to practice rising and falling intonation.

H. EVALUATE With a partner, discuss ways to reduce the cost of your electric bill. What can you do to save energy?

GOAL ■ Create a budget

A. What do you spend money on every month? Make a list.

_____rent_____   _____

_____   _____

_____   _____

_____

B. Share your list with a partner. Add anything to your list that you forgot.

🎧 **C.** **INTERPRET** Listen to Maryanne and Vu talk about their finances. Fill in the missing
CD 1
TR 10
information.

INCOME

Vu's Salary	$4,500
Maryanne's Salary	_____
Total Income	_____

EXPENSES

Rent	_____
Utilities	
Electricity	$100
Gas	_____
Telephone	$125
Cable TV	$125
Internet	$125
Groceries	_____
Auto	
Gas and maintenance	_____
Car loan	_____
Total Expenses	_____

D. Answer the following questions about the Nguyens' budget with a partner.

1. What is their total income?

_____

2. What are their total expenses?

_____

3. How much extra cash do they have left after all the bills are paid? (*Hint:* Subtract total expenses from total income.)

_____

4. In your opinion, what are some things they forgot to budget for?

_____

5. What do you think they should do with their extra money?

_____

E. ILLUSTRATE Look at the bar graph for the Nguyen family's expenses. Complete the graph with their expenses from Exercise C. Write the amounts for any expenses that exceed the chart.

_____ _____

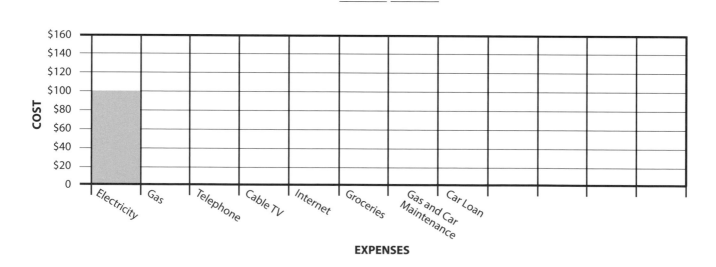

F. Now include on the graph any other items you think the Nguyens should add to their budget and the amount for each.

G. APPLY Work as a team to create a family budget. Use the following information:

- Your family has two adults and three children. The children are two, five, and eight.

- You live in a four-bedroom house that you rent.

- Both adults have full-time jobs.

- You have two cars, one that you own (no payments) and the other that you make payments on.

Decide what your total household income is. Fill in the amounts that you would spend each month on expenses, and make a realistic budget based on your total income.

INCOME
Salary   _____
Salary   _____
Total Income   _____

EXPENSES
Rent   _____
Utilities
    Gas   _____
    Phones   _____
    Cable TV   _____
    Internet   _____
Food
    Groceries   _____
    Dining out   _____
Entertainment   _____
Auto   _____
    Gas and maintenance _____
    Car loan   _____
    Insurance   _____
    Registration   _____

OTHER   _____
_____   _____
_____   _____
_____   _____
_____   _____

Total Expenses   _____

H. ILLUSTRATE Prepare your own personal budget and make a bar graph.

LESSON **5** Tenant rights

GOAL ■ Write a formal letter

A. DETERMINE Look at the pictures. Do you ever have these problems in your home? Are you a do-it-yourself person or do you call someone to make repairs?

a. The air conditioner isn't working.

b. There are roaches and mice in the kitchen.

c. The electricity went out.

d. The faucet is leaking.

B. Who can you call to fix each problem? Match the person with the problem.

1. __c__ electrician

2. _____ handyman

3. _____ exterminator

4. _____ plumber

C. Practice the conversation with a partner. Use the situations in Exercise A to make new conversations.

Tenant: Hello. This is <u>John</u> in Apartment 3B.

Landlord: Hi, <u>John</u>. What can I do for you?

Tenant: <u>The air conditioning in our apartment isn't working</u>. (*State the problem.*)

Landlord: OK. I'll send <u>a handyman over to fix it tomorrow</u>. (*State the solution.*)

Tenant: Thanks.

D. Indira had a bad night in her apartment. Read about what happened.

I had a terrible night. While I was making dinner, I saw a mouse. Then, the electricity went out while I was studying. It was dark, so I went to bed. But I couldn't sleep. The faucet was dripping all night. The neighbors were shouting and their dog was barking, too. Perhaps I should move!

E. Study the charts. Then, underline examples of the *past continuous* in the paragraph in Exercise D.

Past Continuous			
Subject	***be***	**Verb + *ing***	**Example sentence**
I, He, She, It	was	making	I was making breakfast.
You, We, They	were	studying	They were studying.

Use the past continuous to talk about things that started in the past and continued for a period of time.

Past Continuous Using *While*			
Subject	***be***	**Verb + *ing***	**Example sentence**
I, He, She, It	was	making	While I was making dinner, I saw a mouse.
You, We, They	were	studying	The electricity went out while we were studying.

To connect two events that happened in the past, use the past continuous with *while* for the longer event. Use the simple past for the shorter event.
Note: You can reverse the two clauses, but you need a comma if the *while* clause comes first.

F. Use *while* to combine the two sentences. Read the sentences out loud.

1. He was sleeping. The phone rang.
   <u>While he was sleeping, the phone rang. or The phone rang while he was sleeping.</u>

2. Joshua was painting the cabinet. The shelf fell down.
   _____

3. I saw the crack in the wall. I was hanging a painting.
   _____

4. He was taking a shower. The water got cold.
   _____

5. The air-conditioning broke down. We were eating dinner.
   _____

G. Vu Nguyen had a problem when his family first moved into their new apartment. Read the e-mail that he sent to his landlord.

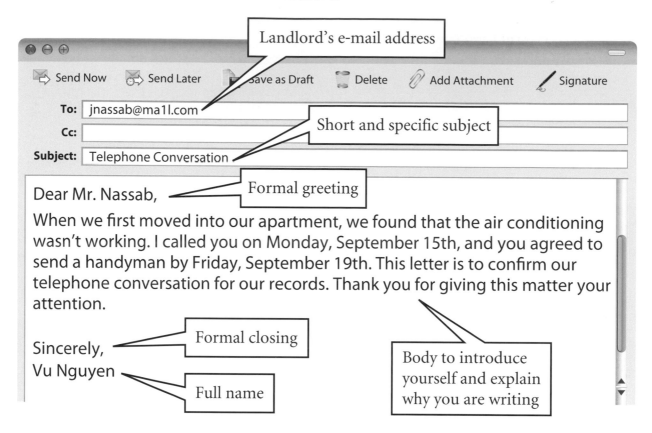

H. What are the different parts of the e-mail? Discuss them with your teacher.

I. **DETERMINE** Work with a partner to brainstorm problems you can have in an apartment and share them with the class.

_____

_____

_____

_____

J. **APPLY** Write an e-mail to your landlord about a problem that you had in the past or a current problem you are having. Use Vu's e-mail as an example.

K. **ANALYZE** Exchange e-mails with a partner. Check your partner's e-mail for grammar, spelling, and punctuation mistakes.

 # How much is the rent?

Before You Watch

A. **Look at the picture and answer the questions.**

1. Who is talking with Naomi?

2. What do you think they are talking about?

While You Watch

B. **Watch the video and complete the dialog.**

Naomi: This is a lot (1) _____*bigger*_____ than the other apartment you showed us.

Landlord: And it's a little (2) _____ expensive, too.

Naomi: How much is the (3) _____?

Landlord: It's $1,700 a (4) _____.

Naomi: Oh.

Landlord: That's typical for this neighborhood. I don't think you'll find anything

(5) _____ around here.

Mateo: Does the rent (6) _____ utilities?

Check Your Understanding

C. **Circle the answer to complete each sentence.**

1. The landlord is showing Hector, Naomi, and Mateo an (apartment/house).

2. The master bedroom is (smaller/bigger) than the other two bedrooms.

3. The rent includes gas and water, but it doesn't include (garbage/electricity).

4. The three friends would prefer an apartment with lower rent and three (bathrooms/bedrooms) that are the same size.

5. The landlord says he has an apartment (downstairs/in another neighborhood) for less rent.

A. Rewrite the classified ad to describe a place where you would want to live.

Three-bedroom apartment with a large kitchen, two-car garage, washer/dryer, and new appliances. Apartment is located near the beach.

$1,500 per month
$500 security deposit   Contact Agent

_____

_____

_____

_____

_____

_____

B. Complete the sentences with *more* or *most* (+) or *fewer, less, fewest,* or *least* (–).

1. (+) Kim's house has _____ *more* _____ entrances than Jen's house.

2. (+) The blue condo has _____ bathrooms than the yellow one.

3. (+) Octavio's apartment gets the _____ light.

4. (–) That condo has _____ balconies than this one.

5. (–) Their house has the _____ furniture.

6. (+) Andrew's place has _____ rooms than Brad's place.

7. (–) The small apartment has _____ patio space than the big one.

8. (+) The Jacksons' apartment has the _____ appliances.

C. Write *yes/no* questions to ask your partner about his or her dream home. Then ask your partner the questions and write the answers.

1 Q: _Do you want four bedrooms?_ _____

A: _No, I don't._ _____

2. Q: _____

A: _____

3. Q: _____

A: _____

4. Q: _____

A: _____

D. Look at the ad you wrote in Exercise A and the answers you got from your partner in Exercise C. Write sentences comparing the two dream homes.

EXAMPLE: _My partner's dream home has fewer bedrooms than my dream home._

1. _____

_____

2. _____

_____

3. _____

_____

4. _____

_____

E. Imagine you are moving to a new city. What utilities will you have to call and order? With a partner, role-play a phone conversation with a customer service representative.

F. **Think about your monthly expenses and complete the budget below.**

INCOME

Salary _____

Total Income _____

EXPENSES

Rent _____

Utilities _____

    Gas _____

    Telephone _____

    Cable TV _____

    Internet _____

Other _____

    Groceries _____

    Dining out _____

    Entertainment _____

Auto _____

    Gas and maintenance _____

    Car loan _____

    Insurance _____

    Registration _____

Total Expenses _____

G. **Use the simple past and the past continuous to complete the sentences.**

1. The light _____*went out*_____ (go out) while Maryanne

   _____*was taking*_____ (take) a shower.

2. A spider _____ (drop) onto my arm while

   I _____ (eat) dinner.

3. While Marie _____ (study), the landlord

   _____ (call).

H. **Think of some problems you have had with the place where you are living. On a piece of paper, use one of your ideas to write a letter to your landlord.**

I. **Highlight ten new words you want to study in the unit. Write the words and definitions on index cards. In pairs, choose a card and ask questions to guess the word on the card.**

With a team, you will create a housing plan, a budget, and a classified ad of where you will live.

1. **COLLABORATE** Form a team with four or five students. Choose positions for each member of your team.

Position	Job description	Student name
Student 1: Leader	Check that everyone speaks English. Check that everyone participates.	
Student 2: Secretary	Write the classified ad.	
Student 3: Financial Planner	Create the budget.	
Students 4/5: Family Representatives	Plan a presentation of your housing plan.	

2. Think about your family's needs. Create your family budget.

3. Think of a place that will be perfect for your family. Create your classified ad.

4. Make a list of all the utilities you will need to arrange for.

5. Create a poster with artwork. Include your budget, classified ad, and list of utilities.

6. Present your poster to the class.

Shipping containers made into temporary housing are perfect for students who live alone.

Living in Isolation

"Everything we depend on
and enjoy has its beginnings
in the natural world ... "
—Paul Colangelo

A. PREDICT Look at the photo of Paul Colangelo. What do you think he is doing?

B. Complete the definitions.

isolation	wildlife	protection	company	habitat

1. A _____ is the natural environment of a living thing.

2. Keeping something safe from harm is _____.

3. _____ is animals that live in the wild.

4. _____ is being alone.

5. Having _____ means having people around; not being alone.

C. **Read about Paul Colangelo.**

> Paul Colangelo is a photographer who has dedicated his life to the protection of wildlife and animal habitats. "I often have to step into the lives of my subjects, so my days often mirror what is normal for others, be it people or wildlife." But what is normal for animals is often not normal for people.
>
> One of Paul's favorite but also most challenging experiences was camping in the Sacred Headwaters of British Columbia, Canada. He lived alone in a large tent for five months over two years to photograph a herd of sheep. Paul didn't have to pay rent, but he had to get permission to camp. And even though he was far away from any towns or cities, his location was very convenient for work. He also had a very large backyard!
>
> While he was camping, a weeklong storm destroyed his tent. He also encountered a pack of 12 wolves, but he wasn't scared. "I saw them not as subjects of study or entertainment, or even amazement, but rather as fellow animals sharing the land."
>
> Many people believe that humans are better than animals. But instead of wildlife and humans being separate living things, Paul believes that people are equal to wildlife. Paul hopes to share this message through his photographs.

D. **Answer the questions on a separate piece of paper.**

1. While photographing sheep, where did Paul live?

2. How many months did Paul spend camping?

3. What animals did Paul see? How many were there?

4. What does Paul believe people are equal to?

E. **ANALYZE** **What do you think Paul is talking about when he says "everything we depend on and enjoy has its beginnings in the natural world . . ."? Share your ideas with a partner.**

_____

_____

_____

F. **Make a list of things you enjoy in nature. Share your list with the class.**

_____

_____

_____

Our Community

Guerilla gardener Ron Finley stands in
an urban garden his team created.

UNIT OUTCOMES

- Ask for information
- Interpret charts and compare information
- Interpret a road map
- Identify daily activities
- Describe a place

Look at the photo and answer the questions.

1. Where is this garden?
2. What do you think the purpose of this garden is?

LESSON **1** Places in your community

GOAL ■ Ask for information

CD 1
TR 11

A. Gloria and her family are new to the community. Read her list of things to do. Where does Gloria need to go for each one? Listen and write the names of the places.

1. Find a place for my children to play sports _____

2. Register for an ESL class _____

3. Open a checking account _____

4. Register my car and get a new license _____

5. Mail some packages back home _____

6. Pick up some bus schedules _____

B. **DEMONSTRATE** Practice the conversation with a partner. Use the information in Exercise A to make new conversations.

Student A: Where can I <u>get a new driver's license</u>?
Student B: At the <u>DMV</u>.

> **DMV**
> DMV = Department of Motor Vehicles

C. Study the chart.

Information Questions		
Location	Where How far What	is the bank? is the school from here? is the address?
Time	When What time How often	does the library open? does the restaurant close? do the buses run?
Cost	How much	does it cost?

D. Match the questions you could ask when calling local businesses with the possible answers.

___g___ 1. How often do the buses run?

a. We open at 10 a.m.

_____ 2. Where's your restaurant?

b. Our store is about five miles away.

_____ 3. How much does it cost?

c. We close at 10 p.m.

_____ 4. What's his address?

d. We're open from 10 a.m. to 6 p.m. on Sunday.

_____ 5. What time do you close?

e. His address is 71 South Pine Avenue.

_____ 6. How far is the store from here?

f. It's on the corner of 7th and Pine.

_____ 7. When do you open?

g. They run every 20 minutes.

_____ 8. What time do you close on Sunday?

h. It costs $50 to service your computer.

E. Practice asking and answering the questions in Exercise D with a partner.

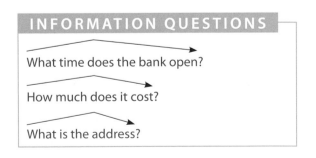

INFORMATION QUESTIONS

What time does the bank open?

How much does it cost?

What is the address?

F. DETERMINE What questions will Gloria need to ask when she calls local businesses? Write questions to match the answers below.

1. _What time does the bank open?_   The bank opens at 9:00 a.m.

2. _____   A driver's license costs $25.

3. _____   The library is about a mile from here.

4. _____   The trains run every ten minutes.

5. _____   You can return books anytime.

6. _____   The DMV is at 112 Main Street.

7. _____   The children's book section is upstairs.

G. Complete the conversations with a logical question or answer. When you are finished, practice the conversations with a partner.

Conversation 1

Student A: Good morning. This is Food Mart.

Student B: _____

Student A: We're open now.

Student B: Great! Thank you.

Conversation 2

Student A: Thank you for calling The Book Stop. How can I help you?

Student B: _____

Student A: 4635 Broadway.

Student B: And when do you close?

Student A: _____

Student B: Thanks!

H. APPLY On a piece of paper, make your own to-do list like the one Gloria made in Exercise A. Next to each item, write the place where you can go in your community to get the task done. Also, write some questions to ask.

To-do	Place	Questions
get information about ESL classes	an adult-education center	When do classes start? Where is the school?

LESSON ② The bank, the library, and the DMV

GOAL ■ Interpret charts and compare information

A. What is the name of your bank? What kind of bank account do you have? Discuss the following words with your classmates and teacher.

ATM	mobile banking	minimum deposit	average daily balance
online banking	debit card	minimum daily balance	unlimited

B. Riverview Bank offers three kinds of checking accounts. Read the brochure below.

Riverview BANK	**Riverview Total Checking**	**Riverview Premier Checking**	**Riverview Premier Plus Checking**
Access to ATMs and branches	yes	yes	yes
Online banking	yes	yes	yes
Mobile banking	yes	yes	yes
Debit card	yes	yes	yes
Fees at non-Riverview ATMs	$2.50 per transaction	$2.50 per transaction	unlimited transactions with no fees
Checks	$5 per box	free standard checks	free personal design checks
Minimum deposit to open	$25	$25	$100
Monthly service fee	$10 or $0 No Monthly Service Fee with: $1,500 minimum daily balance	$25 or $0 No Monthly Service Fee with: $15,000 average daily balance	$25 or $0 No Monthly Service Fee with: $75,000 average daily balance

C. With a partner, practice asking questions about the bank brochure above.

1. What is the minimum deposit to open the _____ account?

2. What is the monthly service fee for the _____ account?

3. Are the checks free with the _____ account?

4. Can you use non–Riverview ATMs for free with the _____ account?

🎧 **D.** **DECIDE** Listen to each person talk about their banking habits. Decide which account above would be best for each one of them.

CD 1
TR 12

E. INFER Read the brochure about library services. Make inferences about the phrases you don't understand.

 MAIN STREET LIBRARY

Library Resources

Circulating materials include hardcover and paperback books, magazines, CDs, books on CD, and DVDs. You can check out these circulating materials for three weeks.

Reference materials include newspapers, encyclopedias, atlases, and other nonfiction books. Reference materials can only be used in the library.

Library Cards

If you want to check out materials from the library, you need a library card. Your first card is free. If you lose it, a replacement card costs $2.

Browse from Home

Use our online library to search for books and then have them sent to your local branch. It takes 2–4 days for a book to arrive at your branch, and you will be sent an e-mail when your book is ready to be picked up.

Fines

If you return materials late or if you lose them, you will have to pay a fine. See the Fine Schedule for more information about lost or overdue materials.

Computers

Use of the computers is free if you have a library card. Printing is based on the number of pages you print.

Renewing Materials

You can keep materials longer than three weeks if you renew them. You can renew them at the library or online using your library card.

Information Services

Librarians can help customers find information, use resources, and suggest books for pleasure reading.

Story Time

Ask a librarian for a schedule. We offer weekly story times for preschool–3rd-grade-aged children.

Other Resources

At the entrance to the library, you will find a resource stand. Here you can find bus schedules, tax forms, and information on English conversation groups. Often there are also discount passes to local attractions.

F. Decide if the statements are true or false based on the information in the library brochure. Change each false statement.

1. You ~~can~~ check out reference materials. *cannot*

2. You can look for books online.

3. You can check out circulating materials.

4. You can use the printer at the library for free.

5. Your first library card costs $2.

6. You can renew materials over the phone using a driver's license.

7. You can check out library materials for three weeks.

8. Circulating materials include books, CDs, DVDs, and encyclopedias.

G. Have you been to the DMV in your city? If so, why did you go there? Did you have to pay for services? Look at the chart of DMV fees below.

	Type	Fee
New	Driver's license	$48
	Learner's permit (valid for 18 months)	$32
	State ID card	$28
	Senior citizen (65 or older) ID card	no fee
Renewal	Driver's license	$48
	State ID card	$28
Replacement	Driver's license	$25
	Learner's permit	$22
	State ID card	$18

H. Read about each person below and write how much they will have to pay.

1. Enrico needs to get a new state ID card. $ _____

2. Liza lost her learner's permit and she needs to get a new one. $ _____

3. Peter's driver's license expired and he needs to get a new one. $ _____

4. Kim and Claudia just learned how to drive and they both need to get new drivers' licenses. $ _____

5. Gertrude is 65 and needs to get a state ID card. $ _____

I. **CREATE** Choose one place in your community: a bank, a library, or the DMV. With a small group, create a one-page information sheet.

A learner's permit is only valid for 18 months.

GOAL ■ Interpret a road map

A. DESCRIBE Discuss the questions with your classmates.

1. How far do you live from your school in miles?

2. What are some major freeways or interstate highways in your area?

3. Where is your school located? What are the nearest towns or cities? Where are they in relation to your school?

B. Look at the key and read the map.

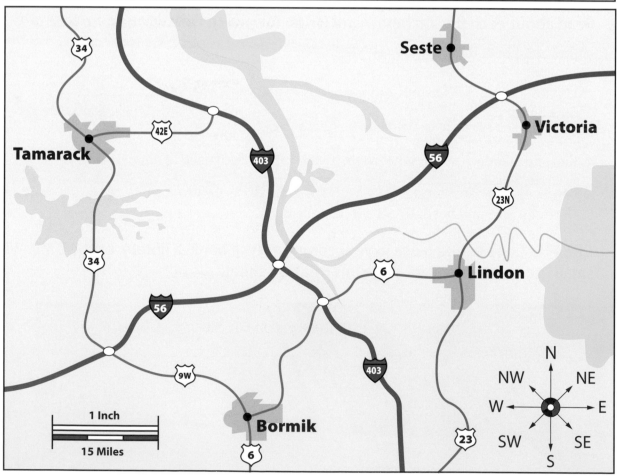

Key		
Compass Points		**Highways**
N - North **NE** - Northeast **E** - East **NW** - Northwest **S** - South **SE** - Southeast **W** - West **SW** - Southwest		Interstate highway State highway

C. **Work in pairs. Choose the correct answers using the map in Exercise B. Then, write one more question and swap books with your partner.**

1. How far is Lindon from Victoria?

   a. 1 mile   b. 15 miles   c. 22.5 miles

2. Which interstate highway is closest to Victoria?

   a. 56   b. 23N   c. 403

3. Where is Tamarack in relation to Lindon?

   a. northwest   b. north   c. west

4. Which direction does Interstate 403 run?

   a. northwest-southeast   b. east-west   c. north-south

5. _____

   a. _____   b. _____   c. _____

D. **DEMONSTRATE** **Study these expressions for giving directions on a road map. Practice pointing with your finger on the map in Exercise B.**

Go north on 403.	**Exit at** Seste.
Take 56 West.	**Get off at** Exit 48 in Bormik.
Get on 34 North.	**Head east** on Route 6.

E. **Using the map in Exercise B, follow the directions below. Which cities are you near?**

1. Take 403 North to 6 East. At Lindon, get on 23 North. Take 23 North and go past Highway 56. What city are you in? _____

2. Take 403 South to 42 East. At Tamarack, take 34 South. Take 56 East to 403 South. Get on Highway 6 going south. What city are you in? _____

3. Take 6 North until it turns into 9 West. Then, get on 56 East. Cross 403 and go about 40 miles. What city is to the south? _____

F. **COMPARE** Look at the city map. How is it different from the map in Exercise B.

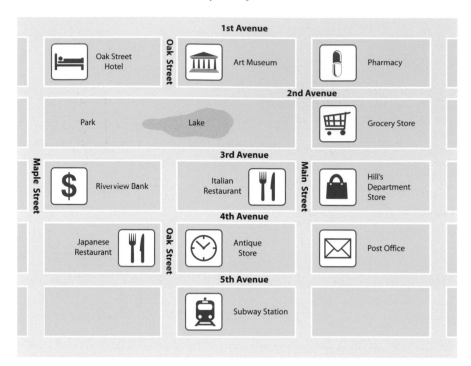

G. Study these expressions for giving directions in a city.

Go straight for three blocks.	It's **next to** the bank.
Turn left. / **Make a** left.	It's **across from** the park.
Take Second Avenue to Oak Street.	It's **on the corner of** First and Main.

H. Read the directions and follow them on the map with your finger.

Start at the subway station on Fifth Avenue. Take a right out of the station. Turn left on Main Street. Go straight for three blocks. Take a left on Second Avenue. It's at the corner of Oak and Second Avenue. What's the name of the building? _____

I. Using the maps in Exercise B and Exercise F, give your partner directions to different places. Start your conversations using the questions below.

	Tamarack		Seste?
	Bormik		Victoria?
How can I get to	the subway station	from	the post office?
	the art museum		the Japanese restaurant?

LESSON ④ Getting things done!

GOAL ▪ Identify daily activities

A. Listen to Gloria talking about her busy morning.

CD 1
TR 13

> Yesterday was a busy day! After I went for an early morning run, I got the kids ready for school. Before my husband left for work, we planned what to cook for dinner. When everyone left the house, I made my list of errands and off I went. First, I returned some books to the library. I stopped by the bank to make a deposit after I returned the books. Then, I went to the post office to mail a package to my family back in Brazil. The next errand on my list was grocery shopping. But, before I went grocery shopping, I remembered to go to the cleaner's and pick up some skirts. And finally, when I finished shopping, I went home.

B. PUT IN ORDER Listen again and number her activities in the correct order.

_____ picked up dry cleaning

_____ got the kids ready for school

_____ planned dinner

_____ went to the bank to make a deposit

___1___ went for a run

_____ made a list of errands

_____ mailed a package at the post office

_____ returned books to the library

_____ went back home

_____ went grocery shopping

The park is a good place to go for a run in the community.

C. *Before, after,* and *when* are used to connect two ideas and show their relationship in time.

Adverbial Clauses with *Before, After,* and *When*	
Rule	**Example sentences**
A comma separates an adverbial clause that comes before the main clause.	**Before I went grocery shopping,** I stopped by the cleaners to pick up some skirts.
	After I returned the books, I stopped by the bank to make a deposit.
	When everyone left the house, I made my list of errands.
A comma is not used when the adverbial clause comes after the main clause.	I stopped by the cleaners to pick up some skirts **before I went grocery shopping.**
	I stopped by the bank to make a deposit **after I returned the books.**
	I made a list of errands **when everyone left the house.**

D. In each of these sentences, underline the action that happened first.

1. After <u>I woke up</u>, I made breakfast.

2. I stopped by the bank to make a deposit before I returned the books.

3. Before Wendy went shopping, she went to the gym.

4. When my kids came home, I made dinner.

E. Rewrite each sentence above, switching the order of the two actions.

1. After I woke up, I made breakfast.

   I made breakfast after I woke up.

2. _____

3. _____

4. _____

F. **ANALYZE** Talk with your partner. In the sentences you wrote above, which action happened first?

G. Write sentences with adverbial clauses. Use the words in parentheses. Then, reverse the clauses and rewrite the sentences.

1. Ali finished work. He went out with his friends. (when)

   a. _When Ali finished work, he went out with his friends._

   b. _Ali went out with his friends when he finished work._

2. Yasu saved enough money. He bought a new bicycle. (after)

   a. _____

   b. _____

3. The alarm went off. Maya jumped out of bed. (when)

   a. _____

   b. _____

4. I cleaned the house. I washed my car. (before)

   a. _____

   b. _____

H. **APPLY** Think of things you did yesterday and the order in which you did them. Write three sentences using *before*, *after*, or *when* to talk about your day.

1. _____
   _____

2. _____
   _____

3. _____
   _____

PAUSING

Pausing is taking a breath in the middle of a sentence.

We usually pause between two thoughts or when there is a comma.

pause

When my kids came home,ⱽ I made dinner.

pause

She went to the storeⱽ before she picked up the dry cleaning.

LESSON ⑤ My town

GOAL ■ Describe a place

A. **Gloria is writing a paragraph about Lindon. Read her brainstorming notes below.**

Reasons I love Lindon

safe neighborhoods (kids play in park)	affordable housing (can buy a new house)
good schools (nationally recognized)	~~good shopping~~
~~mild weather (never gets too cold or hot)~~	good job opportunities (computer industry)

BRAINSTORM
a list of ideas

B. **PUT IN ORDER** **Gloria is writing a paragraph. The six sentences below are not in the correct order. Choose the best topic sentence and write *1*. Choose the best conclusion sentence and write *6*. Then, order the support sentences from *2–5*.**

_____ Thanks to the great job market in Lindon, my husband got an excellent position in a computer company.

_____ Our family can buy a nice house because the housing prices are very affordable here.

_____ I love Lindon so much that I can't imagine moving.

_____ The neighborhoods are very safe, so I can let my children play in the park with other children.

_____ The excellent schools in this area are nationally recognized.

_____ There are many reasons I love Lindon.

C. Compose a paragraph using Gloria's sentences in Exercise B. Use transitions from the box below to connect your support sentences. Write a title for Gloria's paragraph on the top line.

First of all,	Second of all,	Third,	Also,
First,	Second,	Furthermore,	Finally,

_____

_____

_____

_____

_____

_____

_____

_____

_____

D. FORMULATE Now, think about your town. Follow each step below.

1. Brainstorm reasons why you like your town.

Reasons I love _____

friendly people

2. Choose four reasons why you like your town to include in your paragraph.

3. Write a topic sentence for your paragraph.

_____

_____

_____

4. Write four support sentences based on the four reasons you chose.

a. _____

_____

_____

b. _____

_____

_____

c. _____

_____

_____

d. _____

_____

_____

5. Write a conclusion sentence.

_____

_____

_____

E. **COMPOSE** **On a piece of paper, write a paragraph about your town or city using the information in Exercise D. Use transitions to connect your ideas.**

LIFESKILLS ▶ I'd like to open an account

Before You Watch

A. Look at the picture and answer the questions.

1. Where are Naomi and Mr. Sanchez?

2. What are they doing?

While You Watch

B. ▶ Watch the video and complete the dialog.

Mr. Sanchez: You'll receive your (1) _____*checks*_____ in about two weeks. Call me if you don't get them by then.

Naomi: I will. By the way, when will the money be (2) _____?

Mr. Sanchez: Since you (3) _____ cash, the money's available now.

Naomi: Later on, can I open a (4) _____ account online?

Mr. Sanchez: Oh, yes. You can (5) _____ money from your checking account into your savings account any time you like.

Check Your Understanding

C. Put the sentences in order to make a conversation.

_____ **Customer:** A savings account.

_____ **Clerk:** How can I help you?

_____ **Customer:** I'll start with 500 dollars.

_____ **Clerk:** What kind of account would you like to open?

_____ **Customer:** I'd like to open an account.

_____ **Clerk:** How much money would you like to deposit?

Review

Learner Log

I can ask for information.　　I can interpret charts and compare information.
- Yes ■ No ■ Maybe　　■ Yes ■ No ■ Maybe

A. **Where can you do the following things in your community?**

1. have lunch _____

2. get medicine _____

3. mail a letter _____

4. get cash _____

B. **What are some questions you might ask at the places you wrote in Exercise A? Write a question for each place.**

1. _____

2. _____

3. _____

4. _____

C. **Look back at the Riverview Bank brochure on page 89. Read about the following people and decide which checking account would be the best for each.**

1. Vu really wants an account with no service fee. He uses the ATM and doesn't want to pay for ATM transactions. He's saving up to buy a truck, and he has some money in a money market account. All of his accounts total over $30,000.

   Which account is best for Vu?

   _____

2. Mario likes to do his banking online and use the app on his phone. He uses direct deposit and never goes to the ATM. He uses his debit card for most transactions.

   Which account is best for Mario?

   _____

3. Gloria and her husband want to buy a new house. They currently have $15,600 in the bank. Gloria likes to go inside the bank and speak with a teller, but her husband mostly uses the ATM for deposits and withdrawals. Gloria writes lots of checks and likes to personally design her checks.

   Which account is best for Gloria and her husband?

   _____

Learner Log

I can interpret a road map.	I can identify daily activities.
■ Yes ■ No ■ Maybe	■ Yes ■ No ■ Maybe

D. Draw a map showing the way from your school to a nearby restaurant. Then, write the directions. Read the directions to your partner and see if they can draw a map.

E. Write sentences with adverbial clauses. Use *before, after,* or *when*.

1. I woke up. I made breakfast.

   After I woke up, I made breakfast.

2. I got some money out of the ATM. I bought some groceries.

3. Mala finished work. She went to the movies.

4. Luigi graduated from college. He got a job with a computer company.

F. Ask your partner why he or she likes the city he or she lives in. Write four reasons below.

Reasons my partner loves _____

G. Write a short paragraph about your partner's city. Don't forget to use transitions.

H. Share the paragraph with your partner. Have your partner point to the topic sentence, support sentences, and conclusion sentence.

I. Write ten new words you learned in this unit in your notebook. Put them in alphabetical order. Then, look up the new words in a dictionary to see if the order was correct. Write sentences to help you remember the most difficult words.

✔ # Create a community brochure

Imagine that a new family has moved into your neighborhood and you want to tell them all about your community. With your team, create a brochure about your community.

1. **COLLABORATE** Form a team with four or five students. Choose a position for each member of your team.

Position	Job description	Student name
Student 1: Leader	Check that everyone speaks English. Check that everyone participates.	
Student 2: Writer	Write information for brochure.	
Student 3: Designer	Design brochure layout and add artwork.	
Students 4/5: City Representatives	Help writer and designer with their work.	

2. Make a list of everything you want to include in your brochure, for example: information about the library, banks, and other local services.

3. Create the text for your community brochure.

4. Create a map of your community.

5. Create artwork for your community brochure.

6. Present your brochure to the class.

Public sculptures are great places for people to meet in towns and cities.

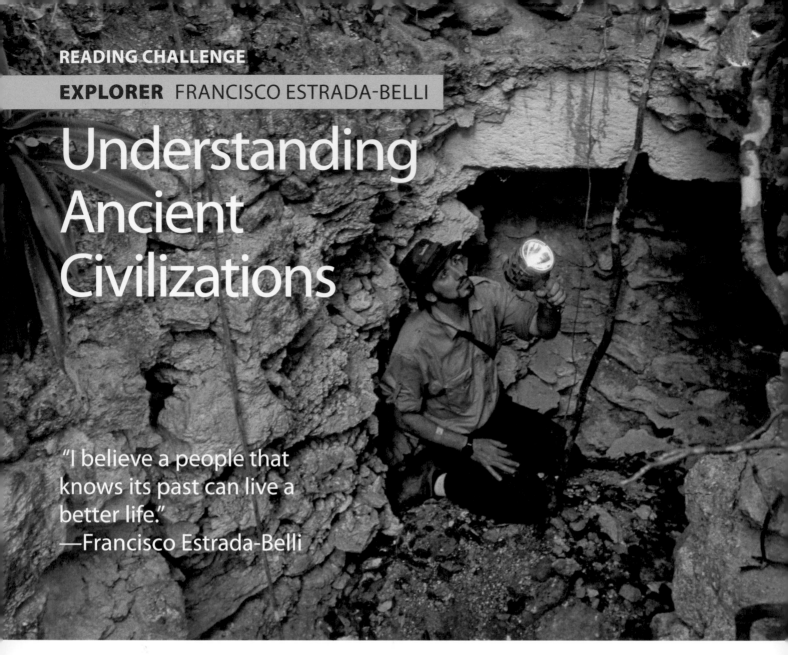

Understanding Ancient Civilizations

"I believe a people that knows its past can live a better life."
—Francisco Estrada-Belli

A. **PREDICT** Look at the photo of Francisco Estrada-Belli. What do you think he is doing?

B. What do you think the words below mean? Match each word to a definition.

1. ancient   a. motivating, stimulating
2. archaeologist   b. very old, usually dating back more than 5,000 years
3. archaeology   c. broken parts of historical buildings that still exist after thousands of years
4. civilization   d. the study of human life and civilizations
5. expedition   e. a journey organized for a specific purpose
6. inspiring   f. a hot, humid area with many trees and plants close together
7. jungle   g. advanced human development
8. ruins   h. a person who studies human life and civilizations

C. Read the interview with Francisco Estrada-Belli.

What did you want to be when you were growing up?

An archaeologist. At age seven, my parents took me to see the Maya ruins of Tikal. I made up my mind then. I've been wanting to answer those same questions I was asking the tour guide since then: How did the Maya build such a great civilization in a jungle? Why did they leave their city?

What inspires you to dedicate your life to study the Maya past?

As a child, it was my dream to explore and study those lost cities in the jungle of Guatemala. It's especially inspiring for me to see the local children learning about their ancient Maya past. I believe a people that knows its past can live a better life.

What's a normal day like for you?

When I'm at home, I teach classes at the university and prepare for the next field expedition. Occasionally, I give newspaper and TV interviews about our work. I have a home office so I can spend some time with my family when I'm not teaching. My two babies wake up early and I get to start my day with them.

When I'm in the field, life is quite different. We camp in the jungle. We get up at dawn (5:30 a.m.), have breakfast in our camp kitchen, and drive in 4x4s a short distance to our dig site. We have lunch at the dig site, work all day, and get back to camp at dusk (5:00 p.m.) for a shower and a nice meal (rice, beans, and chicken, mostly, with lots of hot sauce). We go to bed early.

What do you do in your free time?

I love to spend time with my wife and kids and read archaeology books.

D. On a separate piece of paper, write four sentences about Francisco's day using *before, after,* and *when*.

E. Look at the map. On a separate piece of paper, write Francisco's route from La Libertad to Tikal.

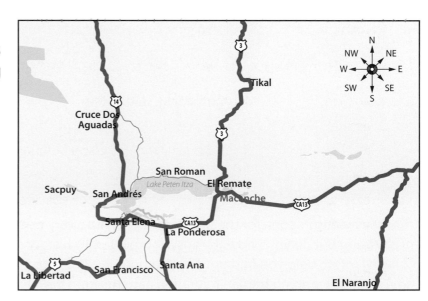

The Human Family Tree

A girl uses a cheek swab to provide DNA.

When we meet someone for the first time, there is one very common question we always ask: *Where are you from?* But do you know the answer? Your family history goes back a very long time and one project wants to help you find out. The Genographic Project is helping people to discover where they come from by mapping human migration patterns from people all over the world.

Before You Watch

A. **Introduce yourself and your family. Complete the chart with the name of each family member.**

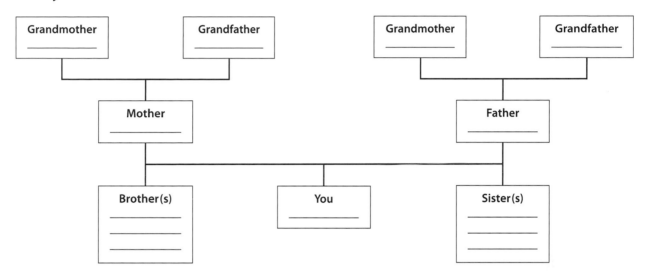

B. **Share the chart from Exercise A with a partner and take turns asking and answering the questions.**

1. Is everyone in your family from the United States?

2. Where does each family member live now?

3. Who in your family looks like you? How are you the same?

C. **Read the words and definitions. Choose the correct answers to complete the sentences.**

roots   the family history of a person
identical   exactly the same
related   in the same family
ancestor   someone in a person's family from the past
genealogy   a study of someone's family history
DNA   material in the body that carries information about how someone looks

1. My sister and I are almost _____. We both have brown hair, blue eyes, and the same height.

   a. identical   b. ancestor   c. DNA

2. Alfredo is _____ to Hector. They are cousins and share two grandparents.

   a. genealogy   b. roots   c. related

3. This person in the photo is our _____. She is my grandfather's grandmother.

   a. genealogy   b. ancestor   c. related

While You Watch

A. Watch the video. Check (✓) the things you see.

_____ A man is waiting at a gas station.　　_____ A woman is taking a picture.

_____ People are waiting in line.　　_____ People are getting cheek swabs.

_____ People are paying money.　　_____ A woman is writing down information.

_____ A man is reading a map.　　_____ A man is carrying a little girl on his shoulders.

B. Match the pictures with the quotations. Then, watch the video again and check your answers.

a.

b.

c.

d.

_____ 1. "The more I know about my past, the more I can understand myself."

_____ 2. "We know where we're from, but we don't really know where we're from."

_____ 3. "My Mom's from South Korea, and on my father's side I am German, Irish, English, and I think a little bit of Native American . . ."

_____ 4. "I am from Madras, the southern part of India. My parents live there, and my grandparents live there . . ."

C. Read the statements and write _True_ or _False_.

1. Genealogy allows us to trace our ancestry.　　_True_

2. A DNA test can trace ancestry back thousands of generations.　　_____

3. Not all humans have DNA.　　_____

4. People adapted to different climates and are varied physically.　　_____

5. Human DNA is almost 100 percent identical.　　_____

After You Watch

A. Read each statement. Choose if you *agree* or *disagree*. Be prepared to discuss with the class.

1. No two humans look the same.

   a. agree   b. disagree

2. Most people want to learn about their ancestors.

   a. agree   b. disagree

3. The more you know about your past the more you can understand yourself.

   a. agree   b. disagree

4. All humans are related.

   a. agree   b. disagree

B. What did you learn about DNA from the video?

1. _We can get DNA samples from a cheek swab._____

2. _____

3. _____

4. _____

5. _____

6. _____

C. Write a paragraph about one of your ancestors. Include interesting details. Share your paragraph in a small group.

EXAMPLE: My grandfather was born in 1922. He was born in Istanbul, Turkey. He was a doctor. He studied medicine in Germany. He lived there and in France for many years. He had five children—four sons and a daughter. He now lives in the United States with his daughter, who is my mother.

_____

_____

_____

_____

Health

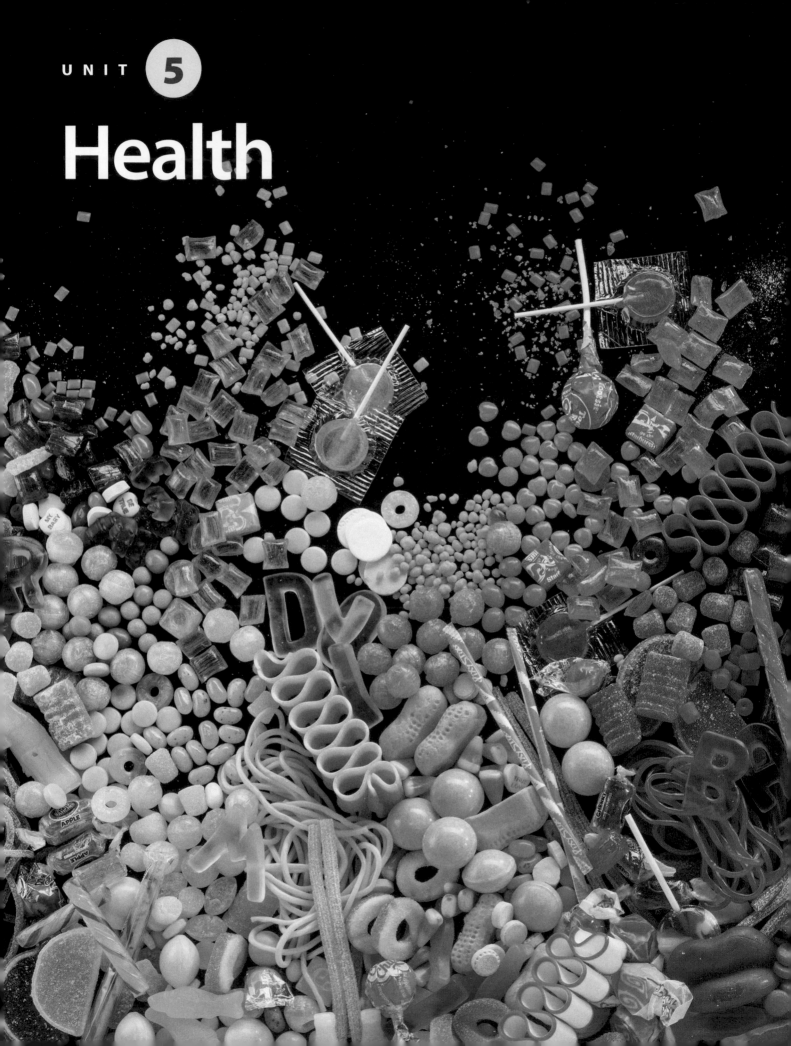

The average American eats 22.7 teaspoons of sugar a day without even touching candy.

UNIT OUTCOMES

- Identify parts of the body
- Communicate symptoms
- Identify and analyze health habits
- Analyze nutrition information
- Interpret fitness information

Look at the photo and answer the questions.

1. What food can you see?
2. Is this food good or bad for you? Why?
3. Which part of the body can this food be bad for?

LESSON **1** The human body

GOAL ▪ Identify parts of the body

A. **Label the parts of the body using the words from the box.**

wrist	hip	~~neck~~	stomach	shoulder	elbow
ankle	knee	chest	finger	toe	chin

1. _____neck_____   2. _____

3. _____   4. _____

5. _____   6. _____

7. _____   8. _____

9. _____   10. _____

11. _____   12. _____

B. **RECALL** **What other parts of the body can you name? Work with a partner. Label other parts of the body by drawing a line from the body part and writing its name.**

C. **Match the doctor with the specialization. Add one more to the list. Go over the pronunciation and answers with your teacher.**

1. __c__ podiatrist
2. _____ dermatologist
3. _____ gynecologist/obstetrician
4. _____ cardiologist
5. _____ ophthalmologist
6. _____ pediatrician
7. _____ dentist
8. _____ allergist
9. _____ psychiatrist
10. _____ _____

a. allergies and asthma
b. children
c. feet
d. teeth
e. mental illness
f. heart
g. eyes
h. women and childbirth
i. skin
j. _____

D. **SUGGEST** **Talk with a partner. Use the statements to make recommendations about which type of doctor to see.**

Student A: My mother's feet hurt.
Student B: She should see a podiatrist.

1. My father is worried about his heart.   _____
2. My six-year-old son has a fever.   _____
3. My nose is running and my eyes are itchy.   _____
4. My eyes hurt when I read.   _____
5. I feel depressed.   _____
6. I have a rash on my neck.   _____
7. I think I have a cavity.   _____
8. _____   _____

E. Look at the illustration of the internal parts of the human body. Review the pronunciation of new words with your teacher.

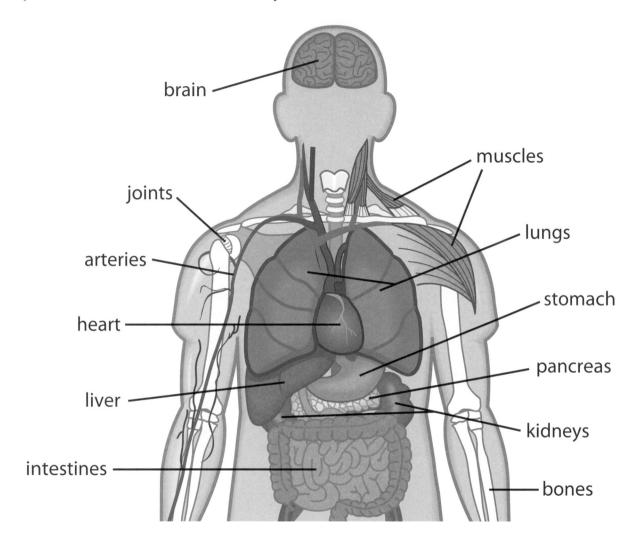

brain

muscles

joints

arteries

lungs

heart

stomach

liver

pancreas

intestines

kidneys

bones

F. Can you talk to your doctor about your medical history? Match the condition or disease with the correct part of the body. Then, add one idea of your own.

1. __b__ high blood pressure

2. _____ asthma

3. _____ ulcers

4. _____ stroke

5. _____ arthritis

6. _____ _____

a. brain

b. heart and arteries

c. joints

d. stomach

e. lungs

f. _____

LESSON **2** Illnesses and symptoms

GOAL ▪ Communicate symptoms

A. Read the conversation and answer the questions.

CD 1
TR 14

Doctor:	What seems to be the problem?
Ali:	I have a terrible backache.
Doctor:	I see. How long have you had this backache?
Ali:	I've had it for about a week.
Doctor:	Since last Monday?
Ali:	Yes, that's right.

1. What is the matter with Ali? _____

2. When did his problem start? _____

B. Practice the conversations. Make new conversations using the pictures below.

Student A: What's the matter?
Student B: I have a headache.
Student A: How long have you had a headache?
Student B: For five hours.

Student A: What's the matter?
Student B: My back hurts.
Student A: How long has your back hurt?
Student B: Since yesterday.

PAST PARTICIPLE	
Base Verb	**Past Participle**
be	been
have	had
feel	felt
hurt	hurt

1. I have a headache.
   (five hours)

2. My eyes are red.
   (last night)

3. My shoulder hurts.
   (two weeks)

4. I feel tired.
   (Monday)

5. My throat is sore.
   (three days)

6. My back hurts.
   (yesterday)

C. Study the chart with your teacher.

Present Perfect					
Subject	*Have*	**Verb**	**Past participle**	**Illness**	**Example sentence**
I, You, We They	have	be feel	been felt	sick ill	I have been sick.
		have	had	a backache a headache	You have had a headache.
He, She, It	has	hurt	hurt	her arm his leg	He has hurt his leg.

Use the present perfect for events starting in the past and continuing up to the present.

D. Complete the sentences with the present perfect.

1. She _____ (be) tired since last week.

2. John's leg _____ (hurt) for three days.

3. Karen _____ (have) a sore throat since last night.

4. I _____ (feel) sick since Monday.

5. The girl's arm _____ (hurt) for two days.

6. The twins _____ (be) sick for a week.

E. Study the chart with your teacher. Complete the sentences with *for* or *since*.

For—length of time	Since—point in time
five minutes	last night
three days	Thursday
one week	November
two years	1998
a long time	I was a child

1. I have been sick _____ Tuesday.

2. The boy's arm has hurt _____ a week.

3. You have felt ill _____ last night.

4. He has had a backache _____ two weeks.

F. **Make sentences using the present perfect and *for* or *since*.**

1. Ali has a backache / Monday

   Ali has had a backache since Monday.

2. I have a cold / three days

   _____

3. my leg hurts / last night

   _____

4. Julie feels dizzy / a week

   _____

5. Peter is sick / two weeks

   _____

G. **DESCRIBE** **Work in pairs. Write symptoms for each illness below.**

Illness	Symptoms
a cold	
the flu	
a cough	
allergies	
depression	

H. **Practice the conversation. Make new conversations. Use the information from the chart in Exercise G.**

Student A: What's the matter?
Student B: I'm coughing and sneezing.
Student A: How long have you been coughing and sneezing?
Student B: I've been coughing and sneezing for a week.
Student A: Do you have a runny nose?
Student B: Yes.
Student A: Sounds like you might have a cold.

LESSON ③ Health habits

GOAL ■ Identify and analyze health habits

A. ANALYZE Look at the picture. What are the people doing? What is healthy and what is unhealthy?

B. Match the health habits with the effects. There may be more than one answer.

1. __j__ be very stressed
2. _____ drink too much alcohol
3. _____ stay in the sun too long
4. _____ eat junk food every day
5. _____ exercise at least three times a week
6. _____ don't get enough calcium
7. _____ don't sleep eight hours every night
8. _____ smoke too much
9. _____ stay away from smoking
10. _____ wear sunscreen

a. have healthy lungs
b. not be well rested
c. damage your liver
d. not have strong bones
e. get lung cancer
f. protect your skin
g. get skin cancer
h. be fit and healthy
i. gain weight
j. have high blood pressure

C. Study the chart with your teacher.

Future Conditional Statements	
Cause: *if* + present tense	**Effect:** future tense
If you *are* very stressed,	you *will have* high blood pressure.
If you *don't get* enough calcium,	you *won't have* strong bones.

We can connect a cause and an effect by using a *future conditional* statement. The *if*-clause (or the *cause*) is in the present tense and the *effect* is in the future tense.

You *will have* high blood pressure   *if* you *are* very stressed.

You can reverse the clauses, but use a comma only when the *if*-clause comes first.

D. Complete the sentences with the correct forms of the verbs in parentheses.

1. If you ____wash____ (wash) your hands a few times a day, you ____won't get____ (not get) so many colds.

2. If Ann _____ (get) her teeth cleaned regularly, she _____ (not have) so many cavities.

3. My dad _____ (not lose) weight if he _____ (keep) eating foods that are high in fat.

4. My skin _____ (burn) if I _____ (not use) sunscreen.

5. If people _____ (not stretch) after they exercise, they _____ (have) sore muscles.

6. Bang Vu _____ (not be able to) talk tomorrow if he _____ (not rest) his voice.

Fast food is cheap and convenient, but it is unhealthy and can make people gain weight.

E. With a partner, practice making conditional statements with the information from Exercise B. Use different subjects (*I, you, we, they, he, she, it*).

1. If we are very stressed, we will have high blood pressure.

2. _____

3. _____

4. _____

5. _____

6. _____

7. _____

F. **EVALUATE** Think about your good and bad health habits. Make two lists.

My good health habits	My bad health habits

G. Write future conditional statements about good health habits you would like to have. Share your ideas with a partner and agree on the four most important ones.

1. If I get more sleep, I will concentrate better on my work.

2. _____

3. _____

4. _____

5. _____

6. _____

LESSON 4 Nutrition labels

GOAL ■ Analyze nutrition information

A. **MyPlate can help you make good decisions about daily food choices. Study the picture and answer the questions.**

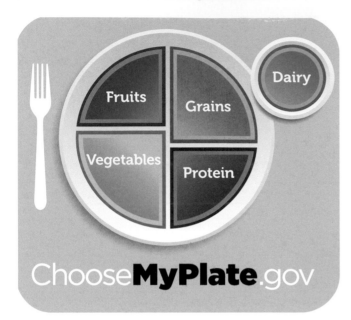

1. Which food group should you eat the most of?

   _____

2. Which food group should you eat the least of?

   _____

B. **Skim the information in the table and answer the questions.**

Fruits	Eat a variety of fresh, canned, frozen, or dried fruit. Limit fruit juice.
Vegetables	Eat a variety of green vegetables like spinach and broccoli. Drink 100% vegetable juice.
Grains	Eat more whole grains. Grains are made from wheat, rice, oats, cornmeal, and barley.
Proteins	Eat a variety of lean proteins. Proteins are meat, poultry, seafood, beans, peas, eggs, nuts, and seeds.
Dairy	Consume dairy to help add calcium to your diet. Dairy products are made from milk.

1. Which food group is rice in? _____

2. Which food group are nuts in? _____

3. What is an example of a green vegetable? _____

4. Why do you think you should limit fruit juice? _____

C. **EVALUATE** Read the tips for healthy eating. Check (✓) the tips you follow or would like to follow. Then, discuss your answers with a partner.

Tips for healthy eating	Follow	Would like to follow
1. Keep raw vegetables in the refrigerator to eat as a snack.		
2. Eat a variety of foods to get all the nutrients you need.		
3. Eat lean meats like fish and chicken.		
4. Choose fat-free or low-fat dairy products.		
5. Try not to drink beverages with a lot of sugar such as soft drinks.		
6. Flavor foods with herbs and spices instead of salt.		
7. Pay attention to serving sizes.		
8. Choose foods that have less saturated fat.		

D. **ANALYZE** Look at the nutrition label for macaroni and cheese.

Macaroni & Cheese Nutrition Facts

Amount Per Serving
Calories 250   Calories from Fat 110

	% Daily Value*
Total Fat 12g	18%
Saturated Fat 3g	15%
Cholesterol 30g	10%
Sodium 470mg	20%
Total Carbohydrate 31g	10%
Dietary Fiber 0g	0%
Sugars 5g	
Protein 5g	
Vitamin A	4%
Vitamin C	2%
Calcium	20%
Iron	4%

*Percent Daily Values are based on a 2,000 calorie diet. Your Daily Values may be higher or lower depending on your calorie needs.

E. Listen to Darla explain nutritional information to her grandmother.

F. Listen to each part of the conversation again and answer the questions. Check (✓) the box next to the correct answer.

1. What does Grandma need to look at if she wants to watch her salt intake?
☐ sodium   ☐ saturated fat

2. How many servings are in this box of macaroni and cheese?
☐ two   ☐ four

3. How many calories should an average adult have each day?
☐ 200   ☐ 2,000

4. What should Grandma avoid to have a healthy heart?
☐ cholesterol and saturated fat   ☐ carbohydrates and saturated fat

5. What should a diabetic look for on a food label?
☐ sugar   ☐ salt

6. What nutrient helps digestion?
☐ iron   ☐ fiber

G. Read the nutrition guidelines and answer the questions about the macaroni and cheese label in Exercise D.

Recommended Amount of Calories and Fat Per Day
- 2,000 calories per day
- 20 or fewer grams saturated fat
- 65 grams total fat

Quick Guide to % Daily Value* for Nutrients
5% or less is LOW   20% or more is HIGH

*Percent Daily Values are based on a 2,000-calorie diet. Your Daily Values may be higher or lower depending on your calorie needs.

1. Is macaroni and cheese high in fat?

2. Is macaroni and cheese low in sodium?

3. Does it contain any protein? How much?

4. What vitamins does it contain? Is it high in vitamins?

5. Is macaroni and cheese a good source of calcium?

6. Do you think macaroni and cheese is a healthy food choice? Why or why not?

H. **PLAN** Work with a partner and plan three meals based on MyPlate in Exercise A.

LESSON ⑤ Healthy living

GOAL ■ Interpret fitness information

A. You are going to read an article about physical fitness. On a separate piece of paper, write one piece of advice that you think it will contain. Then, read the article.

Be physically active each day

Being physically active and maintaining a healthy weight are necessary for good health. Children, teens, adults, and the elderly can improve their health by including moderate physical activity in their daily lives.

Try to get at least 30 minutes (adults) or 60 minutes (children) of moderate physical activity most days of the week, preferably daily.
No matter what activity you choose, you can do it all at once, or spread it out over the day.

Make physical activity a regular part of your routine

Choose activities that you enjoy and that you can do regularly. Some people prefer activities that fit into their daily routine, like gardening or taking extra trips up and down stairs. Others prefer a regular exercise program, such as a physical activity program at their worksite. Some do both. The important thing is to be physically active every day.

Adapted from: Dietary Guidelines for Americans 2000 Center for Nutritional Policy and Promotion, USDA.

B. Decide if the statements are true or false. Check (✓) the correct answers.

	True	False
1. Physical exercise is necessary for good health.	☐	☐
2. Elderly people do not need to exercise.	☐	☐
3. Adults should exercise every day.	☐	☐
4. It is better to exercise throughout the day.	☐	☐
5. Climbing stairs is a good way to exercise regularly.	☐	☐
6. The most important thing is to exercise regularly.	☐	☐

C. Discuss these questions with your partner.

1. Do you exercise more or less than recommended in the article?
2. Does your workplace offer physical activity programs? What are they?

D. Look at the examples of physical activities. Which is an example of a routine activity? Which is an example of a recreational activity?

Mike rides his bicycle to the office every day.

Ana plays tennis twice a week with her friend.

E. Read the list of routine activities. Check (✓) the activities you have tried. Put an *X* next to the activities you would like to try. Add two more activities.

☐ Walk or ride a bike to work.

☐ Walk up stairs instead of taking an elevator.

☐ Get off the bus a few stops early and walk the remaining distance.

☐ Garden.

☐ Push a stroller.

☐ Clean the house.

☐ Play actively with children.

☐ Take a brisk ten-minute walk or bike ride in the morning, at lunch, and after dinner.

☐ _____

☐ _____

F. Read the list of recreational activities. Check (✓) the activities you have tried. Put an *X* next to the activities you would like to try. Add two more activities.

☐ Walk, jog, or cycle.

☐ Swim or do water aerobics.

☐ Play tennis or racquetball.

☐ Golf (pull cart or carry clubs).

☐ Canoe.

☐ Cross-country ski.

☐ Play basketball.

☐ Dance.

☐ Take part in an exercise program at work, home, school, or gym.

☐ _____

☐ _____

G. SUMMARIZE Read the article. Then, discuss the questions below with a partner.

> ### Health Benefits of Physical Activity
>
> Being physically active for at least 30 minutes on most days of the week reduces the risk of developing or dying of heart disease. It has other health benefits as well. No one is too young or too old to enjoy the benefits of regular physical acitivty.
>
> Two types of physical activity are especially benefical:
>
> 1) Aerobic activities: These are activities that speed your heart rate and breathing. They help cardiovascular fitness.
>
> 2) Activities for strength and flexibility: Developing strength may help build and maintain your bones. Carrying groceries and lifting weights are strength-building activities. Gentle stretching, dancing, or yoga can increase flexibility.

1. Why are aerobic activities good for you?
2. What are some examples of aerobic activities?
3. Why are activities for strength good for your bones?
4. What are some examples of strength-building activities?
5. What types of activities can increase your flexibility?
6. What are some activities you do for strength and flexibility?

H. EXPLAIN Read about more benefits of physical activity. Then, discuss the questions with a partner.

> ### More Health Benefits of Physical Activity
>
> ➤ Increases physical fitness
> ➤ Helps build and maintain healthy bones, muscles, and joints
> ➤ Builds endurance and muscular strength
> ➤ Helps manage weight
>
> ➤ Lowers risk factors for cardiovascular disease, colon cancer, and type 2 diabetes
> ➤ Helps control blood pressure
> ➤ Promotes psychological well-being and self-esteem
> ➤ Reduces feelings of depression and anxiety

1. What diseases can exercise help prevent?
2. How does exercise help your circulatory system?
3. How does exercise affect your mood and your mental health?
4. What are some other benefits of exercise?

LIFESKILLS ▶ Exercise is good for you

Before You Watch

A. **Look at the picture and answer the questions.**

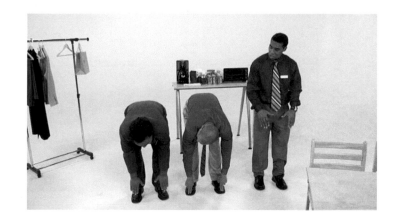

1. Where are Mr. Patel, Hector, and Mateo?

2. What are they doing?

While You Watch

B. ▶ **Watch the video and complete the dialog.**

Mr. Patel: What's (1) _____ *going* _____ on here?

Mateo: We're (2) _____, Mr. Patel. Why don't you join us?

Mr. Patel: I can't do that. I haven't touched my (3) _____ in years.

Mateo: It's (4) _____ for you. C'mon, try it.

Mr. Patel: Well, all right. But not too fast!

Mateo: Don't worry. Let's take it easy. Start by touching your toes. Then, touch your

(5) _____. Finish by putting your hands on your hips.

Check Your Understanding

C. **Match to complete the sentences.**

1. Mateo
2. Exercise
3. Too much sugar
4. Soda and candy
5. Water or juice
6. Mr. Patel

a. are bad for you because they have a lot of calories.

b. are great things to drink after a workout.

c. can create some serious health problems.

d. is not in good shape.

e. has a healthy lifestyle.

f. will prevent your muscles from getting tight.

Review

Learner Log

I can identify parts of the body.   I can communicate symptoms.
■ Yes ■ No ■ Maybe   ■ Yes ■ No ■ Maybe

A. Match each condition with the doctor who treats it. Then, use the information to practice the conversation and make new conversations.

1. __b__ My skin is very red and itchy.   a. dentist

2. _____ My heart is beating quickly.   b. dermatologist

3. _____ My husband is always sneezing.   c. gynecologist/obstetrician

4. _____ My baby is coughing.   d. cardiologist

5. _____ My mother's toe hurts.   e. pediatrician

6. _____ There is something in my eye.   f. ophthalmologist

7. _____ My brother has a cavity.   g. podiatrist

8. _____ I feel nervous all the time.   h. allergist

9. _____ My sister is pregnant.   i. psychiatrist

Student A: <u>My skin is very red and itchy.</u> What should I do?

Student B: You should see a <u>dermatologist</u>.

B. Make sentences using the present perfect and *for* or *since*.

1. Ali has a backache / Monday

   Ali has had a backache since Monday.

2. my neck hurts / two days

   _____

3. Maria feels dizzy / yesterday

   _____

4. my children have a cold / Friday

   _____

5. Peter is sick / two weeks

   _____

6. I have an earache / 10:00 a.m.

   _____

7. they are absent from work / one month

   _____

C. **Complete each future conditional statement.**

1. If you eat out every night, _____ *you will spend a lot of money.* _____.

2. _____ if he goes to the best doctors in the country.

3. If _____, they will look and feel great.

4. If Paulo smokes a pack of cigarettes a day, _____.

5. If _____, you will get sick.

6. If _____, you will improve your flexibility.

7. If you read nutritional labels, _____.

8. If _____, you will have a lot of cavities.

D. **Read the information. Then, decide if the statements below are true or false. Check (✓) the correct answer.**

Find your balance between food and physical activity
- Be sure to stay within your daily calorie needs.
- Be physically active for at least 30 minutes most days of the week.
- About 60 minutes a day of physical activity may be needed to prevent weight gain.
- For sustaining weight loss, at least 60 to 90 minutes a day of physical activity may be required.
- Children and teenagers should be physically active for 60 minutes every day, or most days.

Know the limits on fats, sugars, and salt (sodium)
- Make most of your fat sources from fish, nuts, and vegetable oils.
- Limit solid fats like butter, stick margarine, shortening, and lard, as well as foods that contain these.
- Check the Nutrition Facts label to keep saturated fats, trans fats, and sodium low.
- Choose food and beverages low in added sugars. Added sugars contribute calories with few, if any, nutrients.

	True	False
1. Children need to exercise for only 20 minutes a day.	☐	☐
2. Choose foods that are low in added sugar.	☐	☐
3. If you want to lose weight, you should exercise between 60 and 90 minutes a day.	☐	☐
4. Fish and nuts are good fats.	☐	☐

Learner Log

I can analyze nutrition information. I can interpret fitness information.
■ Yes ■ No ■ Maybe   ■ Yes ■ No ■ Maybe

E. With a partner, ask and answer questions about the nutrition information on the package of frozen peas. Decide if the frozen peas are a healthy choice.

Frozen Peas Nutrition Facts	Amount/Serving	%DV*
Ingredients: green peas, salt	**Total Carbohydrate** 12g	**4%**
Serving size: 2/3 cup (88g)	Fiber 4g	16%
Servings Per Container: About 5	Sugars 6g	
	Protein 5g	
Calories 70	**Vitamin A**	**6%**
Calories from Fat 5	**Vitamin C**	**15%**
Total Fat 0.5g **1%**	**Calcium** 0%	**0%**
Sat. Fat 0g **0%**	**Iron** 4%	**4%**
Cholesterol 0mg **0%**	*Percent Daily Values are based on a 2,000 calorie diet. Your Daily Values may be higher or lower depending on your calorie needs.	
Sodium 100mg **4%**		

1. Are the peas high in fat?
2. Are the peas low in sodium?
3. Do they contain any protein? How much?
4. What vitamins do they contain? Are they high in vitamins?
5. Are the peas a good source of calcium?
6. Do you think peas are a healthy food choice?

F. Look back at the article in Exercise G on page 128. Write two pieces of advice that you would like to follow.

1. _____

2. _____

G. Make a chart in your notebook. Put each word into the correct category. Use a dictionary to check your answers.

ankle	~~ophthalmologist~~	dentist	~~worry~~	~~itchy~~	sore	cavity
stay	hospital	tired cough	diabetes	stress	protect	gain
raw	cholesterol	healthy	active	maintain	gentle	stretch

Noun	Verb	Adjective
ophthalmologist	worry	itchy

✓ **Create a healthy living plan**

You are a team of doctors and health care professionals who have decided to make a healthy living plan to give patients when they leave the hospital.

1. **COLLABORATE** Form a team with four or five students. Choose a position for each member of your team.

Position	Job description	Student name
Student 1: Health Advisor	Check that everyone speaks English. Check that everyone participates.	
Student 2: Writer	Write down information for the plan.	
Student 3: Designer	Design plan layout and add artwork.	
Students 4/5: Health Representatives	Help writer and designer with their work.	

2. Make a list of all the information you want to include in your plan (healthy habits, fitness and nutrition advice, etc.).

3. Create the different sections of your plan, for example, a guide to reading nutritional labels, a guide to exercise, a list of doctors and their specializations, and a guide to common symptoms and diseases.

4. Add artwork to the plan, for example, maps of parks and gyms in your area or a drawing of the food pyramid.

5. Make a collage of all your information.

6. Share your healthy living plan with the class.

Some people in Okinawa, Japan, live healthy lives because they eat locally grown food and practice *hara hachi bu*: eat until you are 80% full.

Blue Zones

"Set up your life, your home environment, your social environment, and your workplace so that you're constantly nudged into behaviors that favor longevity."
—Dan Buettner

A.   **PREDICT** Look at the man waterskiing. How old do you think he is?

B.   Look at the list. Discuss what you think is the most important for long life.

- being active

- spending time with family and friends

- living in an isolated city

- having a sense of humor

- eating healthy food

An elderly man waterskiing on a river.

C. Read about Dan Buettner.

What would you say if someone told you that by making a few changes in your life, you could live longer and spend less time at the doctor's office? Dan Buettner, internationally recognized researcher, explorer, and *New York Times* best-selling author, has been trying to find a way. He has been searching for *Blue Zones*. These are groups of people or parts of the world where people live longer.

One Blue Zone that Dan has researched is Sardinia, Italy. Sardinians live longer than most people. In fact, Sardinia has ten times more centenarians (people who have lived to 100 years old) than the United States. One of the reasons that this continues to be true is that Sardinia is a very <u>isolated</u> island, which means their genes have stayed pure. In addition to being geographically isolated, Sardinians are culturally isolated as well. This has led to a very traditional lifestyle: family is important, their food is <u>locally grown</u>, and physical activity is a part of daily life. Today, they hunt, fish, and harvest their food in the same way they have always done. They eat a diet high in omega-3 fatty acids, which possibly helps protect them from heart <u>disease</u> and <u>Alzheimer's</u>*. They are very close with their family and friends, and social gatherings are important. <u>Elders</u> are always <u>celebrated</u> and <u>laughter</u> helps <u>reduce their stress</u>. They use their legs for transportation and their bodies for physical labor, keeping them physically fit. All of these lifestyle characteristics contribute to Sardinians being part of the Blue Zone.

In 2009, Dan was part of a project that tested these characteristics in Albert Lea, Minnesota. The result? They successfully raised life expectancy and lowered health care costs by almost 40 percent.

Think about it, if you follow these lifestyle characteristics yourself, you will live longer!

* Alzheimer's: disease that leads to memory loss

D. ANALYZE Discuss the vocabulary below. Which words are positive? Which words are negative? Which words are neither positive nor negative? Why?

Alzheimer's	elders	locally grown
celebrated	isolated	reduce stress
disease	laughter	

E. *Life expectancy* is how long people are expected to live. What do you think Dan Buettner's Blue Zone principles are that raised the life expectancy in Minnesota? Discuss with a small group and make a list on a separate piece of paper.

UNIT 6

Getting Hired

Three National Park rangers use a virtual kiosk that helps visitors interact with parks around the country.

UNIT OUTCOMES
- Identify job titles and skills
- Identify job skills and personality traits
- Interpret job advertisements
- Complete a job application
- Interview for a job

Look at the photo and answer the questions.

1. What job title do you think the women have?
2. What skills do they need to do their job?

LESSON ① Jobs and careers

GOAL ▪ Identify job titles and skills

A. Look at the photos and write the correct letter for each job.

a.

b.

c.

d.
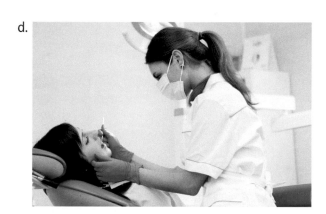

Job	Letter
graphic designer	_c_
dental hygienist	_____
home health aide	_____
accountant	_____

B. ANALYZE Talk to your partner about the four jobs in Exercise A. Which job is the most interesting? Which job is the most difficult? Why?

C. Match the job with the description.

_____ 1. graphic designer   a. cleans teeth

_____ 2. repair technician   b. takes care of children

_____ 3. administrative assistant   c. designs and maintains yards

_____ 4. dental hygienist   d. writes programs for computers

_____ 5. landscaper   e. designs artwork for companies

_____ 6. accountant   f. does general office work

_____ 7. home health aide   g. uses equipment in a factory or on a construction site

_____ 8. computer programmer   h. keeps financial records

_____ 9. nanny   i. fixes appliances and equipment

_____ 10. machine operator   j. takes care of sick people in their own homes

D. Look at the pictures. What do you think each person does? Write a job title.

doctor	electrician	server	judge
~~lawyer~~	plumber	scientist	postal worker

1. ____lawyer____ 2. _____ 3. _____ 4. _____

5. _____ 6. _____ 7. _____ 8. _____

E. IDENTIFY Work in a small group to write one skill for each job title.

1. doctor _____

2. server _____

3. judge _____

4. postal worker _____

F. Work in a small group again to write the job title for each skill.

1. _____ fixes leaking pipes

2. _____ fixes electrical problems

3. _____ studies or practices law

4. _____ invents new medicine

G. Practice the conversation with a partner. Use the job titles and skills from this lesson to make new conversations.

Student A: What does a graphic designer do?
Student B: A graphic designer makes artwork for companies.

H. Work with a partner. Think of more jobs and write what each person does.

1. A farmer grows fruits and vegetables. _____

2. _____

3. _____

4. _____

5. _____

6. _____

7. _____

8. _____

LESSON **2** What can you do?

GOAL ■ Identify job skills and personality traits

A. EVALUATE What are your job skills? Check (✓) the things you are good at. Add two skills to the list.

- ☐ answer phones and take messages
- ☐ assemble things
- ☐ cook
- ☐ draw
- ☐ drive a car or truck
- ☐ fix machines
- ☐ order supplies
- ☐ balance accounts
- ☐ operate machines
- ☐ talk to customers

- ☐ read maps
- ☐ sew
- ☐ speak other languages
- ☐ take care of children
- ☐ take care of the elderly
- ☐ type
- ☐ repair computers
- ☐ use computers
- ☐ _____
- ☐ _____

B. Write two skills you want to improve and two skills you want to learn.

Skills I want to improve	Skills I want to learn

C. Work with a partner. Think of ways your partner can learn or improve the skills he or she wrote in Exercise B. Use ideas from the box and make suggestions for your partner.

volunteer	ask a friend to teach you	practice at home
take an evening class	take an online class	do training at your company

Student A: I want to learn how to <u>take care of the elderly</u>.
Student B: Maybe you could <u>volunteer at a hospital or nursing home</u>.

D. **SUGGEST** Claude needs a job. Can you suggest two for him?

> Claude is quiet and shy. He is friendly, but he doesn't really like to talk to customers. He is very good at assembling things. When he was a teenager, he enjoyed fixing bicycles. He likes to be busy. He wants to get a job where he can use his technical skills.

1. _____

2. _____

E. Study the chart with your classmates and teacher. Then, underline examples of infinitives and gerunds in the paragraph in Exercise D.

Infinitives and Gerunds Infinitive = *to* + verb Gerund = verb + *ing*			
Verb	**Infinitive or gerund**	**Example sentence**	**Other verbs that follow the same rule**
want	infinitive	He wants *to get* a job.	plan, decide
enjoy	gerund	He enjoys *fixing* bicycles.	finish, give up
like	both	He likes *to talk*. He likes *talking*.	love, hate

Some verbs take the infinitive and some verbs take the gerund. There are even some verbs that take both.

F. Are these verbs followed by an infinitive, a gerund, or both? Check (✓) the correct answers.

1. I like _____ on a team.   ☐ to work   ☐ working   ☑ to work/working

2. I enjoy _____ problems.   ☐ to solve   ☐ solving   ☐ to solve/solving

3. I want _____ to customers.   ☐ to talk   ☐ talking   ☐ to talk/talking

4. I decided _____ math.   ☐ to study   ☐ studying   ☐ to study/studying

5. I hate _____ decisions.   ☐ to make   ☐ making   ☐ to make/making

6. I gave up _____ two years ago.   ☐ to smoke   ☐ smoking   ☐ to smoke/smoking

7. I love _____ machines.   ☐ to fix   ☐ fixing   ☐ to fix/fixing

G. EVALUATE What kind of personal skills do you have? Check (✓) the ones that describe you and add more skills to the list.

☐ solve problems   ☐ help people

☐ work under pressure   ☐ organize information

☐ work in a fast-paced environment   ☐ work with money

☐ work on a team   ☐ talk to customers

☐ make decisions   ☐ _____

☐ pay attention to details   ☐ _____

☐ work with my hands   ☐ _____

☐ read and follow directions   ☐ _____

H. Study the chart with your classmates and teacher.

Gerunds and Nouns after Prepositions					
Subject	**Verb**	**Adjective**	**Preposition**	**Gerund/Noun**	**Example sentence**
I	am	good	at	fixing bicycles	I am good at *fixing bicycles.*
She	is	good	at	math	She is good at *math.*

A gerund or a noun follows an adjective + a preposition. Some other examples of adjectives + prepositions are *interested in, afraid of, tired of, bad at,* and *worried about.*
When a noun is plural, it is also common to use the preposition *with: I am good with customers.*

I. Tell your partner about your skills and interests. What things are you *good at, bad at, interested in, tired of,* and *afraid of*? Your partner will suggest a good job for you.

Student A: I'm good at <u>paying attention to details</u>. I'm interested in <u>organizing information</u>.
Student B: Maybe you should be <u>an accountant</u>.

J. APPLY Write a paragraph about your job skills. Describe the job skills you have or are interested in learning. Say why these skills are important and useful.

_____

_____

_____

_____

_____

LESSON ③ Help wanted

GOAL ■ Interpret job advertisements

A. Read the following job advertisements.

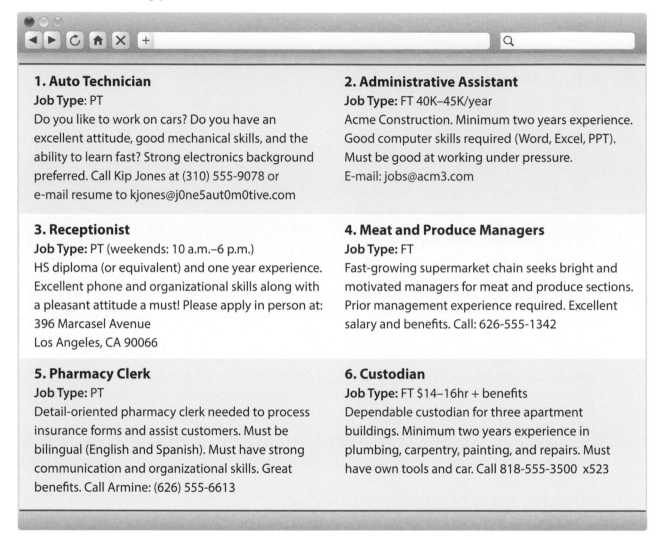

1. Auto Technician
Job Type: PT
Do you like to work on cars? Do you have an excellent attitude, good mechanical skills, and the ability to learn fast? Strong electronics background preferred. Call Kip Jones at (310) 555-9078 or e-mail resume to kjones@j0ne5aut0m0tive.com

2. Administrative Assistant
Job Type: FT 40K–45K/year
Acme Construction. Minimum two years experience. Good computer skills required (Word, Excel, PPT). Must be good at working under pressure.
E-mail: jobs@acm3.com

3. Receptionist
Job Type: PT (weekends: 10 a.m.–6 p.m.)
HS diploma (or equivalent) and one year experience. Excellent phone and organizational skills along with a pleasant attitude a must! Please apply in person at:
396 Marcasel Avenue
Los Angeles, CA 90066

4. Meat and Produce Managers
Job Type: FT
Fast-growing supermarket chain seeks bright and motivated managers for meat and produce sections. Prior management experience required. Excellent salary and benefits. Call: 626-555-1342

5. Pharmacy Clerk
Job Type: PT
Detail-oriented pharmacy clerk needed to process insurance forms and assist customers. Must be bilingual (English and Spanish). Must have strong communication and organizational skills. Great benefits. Call Armine: (626) 555-6613

6. Custodian
Job Type: FT $14–16hr + benefits
Dependable custodian for three apartment buildings. Minimum two years experience in plumbing, carpentry, painting, and repairs. Must have own tools and car. Call 818-555-3500 x523

B. Are there any words or abbreviations that are new to you? List them below and discuss them with your classmates and teacher.

_____ _____ _____

_____ _____ _____

_____ _____ _____

C. INTERPRET Read the ads in Exercise A again and answer the questions below.

1. What experience should the auto technician have? _____ *electronics background* _____

2. Which employer wants someone who can work under pressure? _____

3. Which job requires a friendly personality? _____

4. Which job requires a car? _____

5. Which job requires someone who is detail-oriented? _____

6. Which job requires someone who is bilingual? _____

7. What are ways to apply for these jobs? _____

D. What skills are required for each job advertised in Exercise A? Complete the table.

Job	Skills required or preferred
Auto technician	
Administrative assistant	
Receptionist	
Meat and produce managers	
Pharmacy clerk	
Custodian	

E. DETERMINE Read the descriptions and decide which job or jobs from Exercise A each person should apply for. Write the job titles.

1. Lance recently moved here and needs to find a job. At his old job, he answered the phone, scheduled meetings, and sent memos. He would like a job doing the same thing. Which job or jobs should he apply for?

   _____

2. Kyung was recently laid off from his janitorial job at the local school district. He had been working there for ten years and took care of all the maintenance and repairs for the school. Which job or jobs should he apply for?

   _____

3. Kim wants to find some extra work on the weekends. She is good at answering phones and she is very organized. Which job or jobs should she apply for?

   _____

4. Rita manages a bakery but wants to find a job closer to home. She is smart and willing to work hard. She really likes to work with people and would like to find a job in the same line of work. Which job or jobs should she apply for?

   _____

F. EVALUATE Answer the following questions about yourself.

1. Which job advertised in Exercise A is best for you? Why?

   _____

2. Which job would you most like to have? Why?

   _____

3. Which job would you like the least? Why?

   _____

G. CREATE On a separate piece of paper, write an ad for your dream job. Include the job title, skills, preferences, pay, and any other necessary information.

LESSON ④ Employment history

GOAL ■ Complete a job application

A. DETERMINE Look at the ways people apply for jobs. How did you get your last job? What's the best way to get a job? Discuss your answers with a partner.

- know someone at a company (personal connection)
- go to an employment agency
- reply to a classified ad
- see a *Help Wanted* sign and fill out an application
- introduce yourself to the manager and fill out an application
- send a resume to a company

B. Not every business advertises available positions. If you want to work somewhere, you should go in and ask for an application. Read the conversation below.

Ramona:	Excuse me. May I speak to the manager, please?
Employee:	She's not here right now. Can I help you?
Ramona:	Are you hiring?
Employee:	As a matter of fact, we are.
Ramona:	What positions are you hiring for?
Employee:	We need a <u>manicurist</u> and a <u>receptionist</u>.
Ramona:	Great. Can I have an application, please?
Employee:	Here you go. You can drop it off any time.
Ramona:	Thanks a lot.
Employee:	Sure. Good luck.

C. Practice the conversation in Exercise B. Use the job titles from this unit to make new conversations.

D. On a job application, you have to fill out certain information. Match the type of information to its description.

__c__ 1. Personal Information   a. people you have worked with

_____ 2. Employment History   b. previous jobs you had

_____ 3. Availability   c. name, address, skills

_____ 4. Education   d. schools you attended

_____ 5. References   e. when you are free to work

E. ANALYZE Look at Ramona's job application. Discuss the sections with your classmates.

SECTION 1: PERSONAL INFORMATION	
Name: Ramona Jimenez	
Address: 123 Stanford Avenue, Garden Grove, CA 92840	
Telephone: (714) 555-9765	**E-mail address:** rjimenez@ma1l.com
Position applied for: Manicurist	
Employment Desired (Circle) (Full-time) Part-time Both	How many hours can you work a week? ___40___ Can you work nights? (Circle) Yes (No) When are you available to start? ___ASAP___

SECTION 2: EMPLOYMENT HISTORY				
Employer	**Employment dates**	**Pay or salary**	**Job position**	**Reason for leaving**
Carly's	1/2015–2/2016	Minimum wage + tips	Server	Moved
Bill's Burgers	5/2012–1/2015	Minimum wage	Server	Promotion

SECTION 3: EDUCATION HISTORY				
Type of school	**School name**	**Location**	**Number of years completed**	**Major or degree**
College	Long Beach City College	Long Beach, CA	1	
High school	Los Alamitos High School	Los Alamitos, CA	4	diploma

F. Listen to the rules for filling out an application. Fill in the blanks.

CD 1 TR 16

1. Use a dark _____, blue or _____ ink.

2. Don't _____ any mistakes. Use correction fluid to

   _____ any mistakes.

3. Answer every _____. If the question doesn't apply to you, write

   _____ (Not Applicable).

4. Tell the _____! Never _____ on your job application.

5. Don't _____ or wrinkle the application.

6. Keep the application _____—no food or coffee stains!

7. Write as _____ as possible. _____ it if you can.

8. If you don't _____ the question, ask someone before you answer it.

G. Fill out the job application with your own information.

SECTION 1: PERSONAL INFORMATION		
Name:		
Address:		
Telephone number:	**E-mail address:**	
Position applied for:		

Employment Desired (Circle) Full-time Part-time Both	**Days available to work (Circle)**	
	No preference	Thursday
	Monday	Friday
	Tuesday	Saturday
	Wednesday	Sunday

SECTION 2: EMPLOYMENT HISTORY				
Employer	**Employment dates**	**Pay or salary**	**Job position**	**Reason for leaving**

SECTION 3: EDUCATION HISTORY				
Type of school	**School name**	**Location**	**Number of years completed**	**Major or degree**

SECTION 4: REFERENCES			
Name	**Position**	**Company**	**Contact details**

I hereby certify that the above information is true to the best of my knowledge. I authorize previous employers to provide any information they feel appropriate.

Signature _____

LESSON 5 Why do you want to work here?

A. Have you ever had a job interview? What happened? Tell your partner.

B. During a job interview, an employer will try to find out about an applicant's character and personality. Read and listen to find out what interviewers look for during an interview.

CD 1
TR 17

> Your job interview is the most important part of the application process. This is when the employer gets to meet you and learn more about you. Employers are interested in your skills and experience, but they also look for personality and character traits.
>
> **Do you stand tall and smile confidently?** Employers will notice your self-confidence. Managers want to hire employees who have confidence in themselves and will have confidence in the job they are doing.
>
> **Do you like to work hard and do a good job?** Another important thing an interviewer looks for is enthusiasm about work. People who are enthusiastic about a job make great employees. They are happy with the work and usually stay with the company for a while.
>
> **Are you friendly and easy to talk to?** Do you pay attention to how other people are feeling? Warmth and sensitivity are also very important traits. A person with these characteristics will make a good coworker; someone who can work well with others.
>
> Do you have some or all of these traits? Can you show that you have these traits in an interview? If the answer is *yes*, you will have a good chance of getting the job.

C. EXPLAIN Discuss the following questions with a partner.

1. In your opinion, which is the most important trait: self-confidence, enthusiasm, or a friendly personality?

2. According to the information in Exercise B, how can you use body language to show you are self-confident? Can you think of any other ways you can show confidence through body language?

3. How can you show an employer that you are enthusiastic about a job and a company?

4. According to the information, why do employers like to hire warm, sensitive people?

5. Do you think there are other character traits that employers like? What are they?

D. Imagine you are interviewing someone for a job as an administrative assistant in a busy doctor's office. List six personality traits you would look for.

honest	confident	funny	friendly	sensitive	thoughtful	enthusiastic
arrogant	motivated	warm	helpful	careful	intelligent	sneaky

1. _____   2. _____   3. _____

4. _____   5. _____   6. _____

E. **DETERMINE** Discuss what clothing and accessories are appropriate or not appropriate for a job interview. Fill in the chart with your ideas.

Men	Appropriate	Not appropriate
	long-sleeved shirt	t-shirt

Women	Appropriate	Not appropriate

F. **Study the chart with your classmates and teacher.**

Would rather					
Subject	*would rather*	**Base form**	*than*	**Base form**	**Example sentence**
I, You, She, He, It, We, They	would ('d) rather	work alone	than	work with people	I would rather work alone than work with people.

Note: You can omit the second verb if it is the same as the first verb: *I would rather work nights than (work) days.*

G. **Which work situation do you prefer? Talk to your partner about your preferences.**

Student A: Would you rather work inside or outside?
Student B: I'd rather work inside because I hate the cold.

1. work alone / on a team

2. work days / nights

3. get paid hourly / weekly

4. have your own business / work for someone else

5. retire at 65 / work until you are 70

6. walk to work / drive to work

H. **Write sentences about your ideal work situation.**

1. *I'd rather work on a team than alone because I like talking to people.*

2. _____

3. _____

I. **PREPARE Imagine you are preparing for a job interview. Choose a job from the ads on page 144 or one of your own. Work with a partner and answer the questions below.**

1. What are your skills?

2. Why do you think you would be good at this job?

3. How would you describe your personality?

4. What did you like and dislike about your last job?

5. Would you rather work full-time or part-time?

6. What salary do you expect?

▶ **How's your new job, Hector?**

Before You Watch

A. **Look at the picture and answer the questions.**

1. Where are Hector, Naomi, and Mateo?

2. What is Naomi doing with the chocolates?

While You Watch

B. ▶ **Watch the video and complete the dialog.**

Hector: I just feel I could be (1) _____ doing _____ something more. So, I applied for a job at the school newspaper.

Naomi: Wow, that's really (2) _____. Do you really have time for two jobs?

Hector: Well, I'd have to (3) _____ on my hours at the store. Mr. Patel might not like that. He might fire me, and then I'll be poor, and then my parents will get mad, and they'll kick me out and …

Mateo: Just tell Mr. Patel it'll get him some extra publicity. Tell him you're going to write a news article about him. He won't (4) _____ you. He'll love you even more.

Naomi: Mateo is right. Everything will be fine. If that's what you want to do, you (5) _____ go for it.

Check Your Understanding

C. **Write *newspaper* or *clothing store* next to the pros.**

1. going different places _____ newspaper _____

2. working there with Mateo _____

3. meeting interesting people and getting paid for it _____

4. learning lots of new things _____

5. leading to a career _____

6. working at a more interesting job _____

Review

A. Read each skill below and write the correct job title on the line.

1. cleans teeth _____

2. sends memos, files, and does general office work _____

3. takes a patient's temperature and blood pressure _____

4. fixes pipes _____

5. cleans office buildings _____

6. operates machinery _____

7. takes care of children _____

8. maintains yards _____

B. List six job skills you have.

1. _____

2. _____

3. _____

4. _____

5. _____

6. _____

C. Complete the sentences using the gerund or an infinitive form of the verb in parentheses.

1. I like _____ on a team. (work)

2. I am good at _____ to customers. (talk)

3. They hate _____ the phone. (answer)

4. I decided _____ a computer course next semester. (study)

5. He is interested in _____ cars. (repair)

6. We finished _____ our reports yesterday. (write)

Learner Log

I can interpret job advertisements. I can complete a job application.

☐ Yes ☐ No ☐ Maybe   ☐ Yes ☐ No ☐ Maybe

D. Read the job ads.

◄ ► ↻ ⌂ ✕ ＋ [   ] 🔍

1. Administrative Assistant
FT: 10 a.m. – 6 p.m.
Requires HS diploma and one-year experience.
Excellent phone and organizational skills along
with a pleasant attitude a must! Please send
resume to: jobs@aaj08s.com

2. Custodian
Reliable custodian for local school district.
Minimum one-year experience cleaning,
plumbing, carpentry, painting, and repairs.
Will provide supplies and tools.
$12–14/hr + benefits.
Call: (818) 555-6879.

E. Look at the ads in Exercise D. Write: *administrative assistant, custodian,* or *both.*

1. Which job requires experience?   _____

2. Which job requires a high school diploma? _____

3. Which job offers benefits?   _____

4. Personality is NOT important for which job? _____

F. Fill out the partial job application.

SECTION 1: PERSONAL INFORMATION	
Name:	
Address:	
Telephone number:	**E-mail address:**
Position applied for:	
Employment Desired (Circle) Full-time Part-time Both	How many hours can you work a week? _____ Can you work nights? (Circle) Yes/No When are you available to start? _____

SECTION 2: EMPLOYMENT HISTORY				
Employer	**Employment dates**	**Pay or salary**	**Job position**	**Reason for leaving**

SECTION 3: EDUCATION HISTORY				
Type of school	**School name**	**Location**	**Number of years completed**	**Major or degree**

G. What kind of personality traits should people have for these jobs? Write two adjectives for each job. Share your answers with a partner.

1. home health aide: *responsible, caring* _____

2. manager in a clothing store: _____

3. receptionist in a dentist's office: _____

4. nanny: _____

5. custodian in a school: _____

6. teacher: _____

H. Write six interview questions for one of the following jobs. Interview a partner.

landscaper	receptionist	furniture store manager	computer technician
bookkeeper	waiter	assembler in a factory	home health aide

1. _____

2. _____

3. _____

4. _____

5. _____

6. _____

I. Dictionaries use different symbols to show word stress. Look up the following words in the dictionary. Write them with the correct syllable stress.

1. applicant *aP-pli-cant* _____

2. previous _____

3. bookkeeper _____

4. technician _____

5. computer _____

6. equipment _____

7. environment _____

8. require _____

Create a job application portfolio

With your team, you will plan the contents and layout for a job application portfolio. Each student will create his or her own job application portfolio.

What does a job application portfolio include?

- a job application information sheet
- a list of rules for filling out a job application
- a list of skills
- sample interview questions and answers
- certificates

- awards
- transcripts
- performance reviews
- letters of recommendation

---

1. **COLLABORATE** Form a team with four or five students. Choose a position for each member of your team.

Position	Job description	Student name
Student 1: Leader	Check that everyone speaks English and participates.	
Student 2: Secretary	Write a list for what your job portfolio should include.	
Student 3: Designer	Design order of job application portfolio.	
Students 4/5: Member(s)	Help secretary and designer with their work.	

2. Make a list of all the information you want to include in your portfolio. Look at the list above for help. Decide how many pages you will need.

3. With your team, decide the best order for your portfolio.

4. Collect and create items to put in your individual portfolio. Put your portfolio together.

5. Share your portfolio with at least two other students.

6. Set up an interview with your teacher and share your portfolio with him or her.

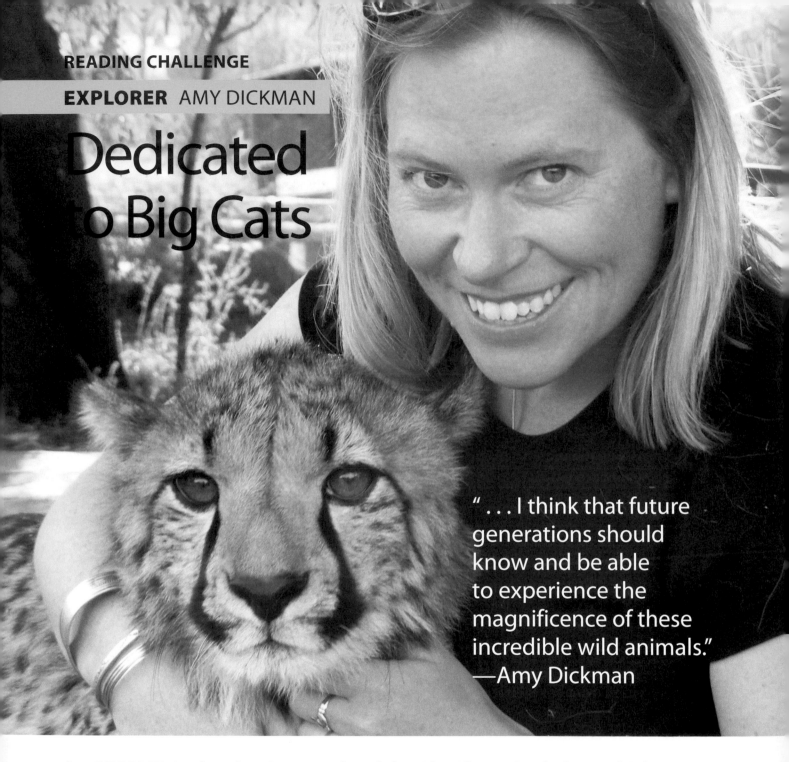

Dedicated to Big Cats

" . . . I think that future generations should know and be able to experience the magnificence of these incredible wild animals."
—Amy Dickman

A. PREDICT Look at the picture and read the title. What animals do you think Amy works with?

B. Amy Dickman is an animal conservationist. Write four job skills you think she has.

_____   _____

_____   _____

C. SKIM Skim the first paragraph of the article. What do you think it will be about?

D.   Read about Amy Dickman.

> Big cats have always fascinated Amy Dickman. When she was ten years old, she wrote down that at the age of 30, she wanted to be working in Tanzania with big cats. And that's exactly what she is doing! At first, she considered becoming a vet, but she decided that she would rather protect these animals than care for them in a clinic.
>
> When she was still in school, she started working at local zoos. Later, while she was getting her undergraduate degree in zoology, she volunteered at Chester Zoo and did a research project on their cheetahs. Once she graduated, she got a job at the Wildlife Conservation Research Unit at Oxford University. This research unit sent her to Namibia, where she spent almost six years working with big cats in the wild.
>
> At her job, Amy does a variety of things and not all of them are working with cats. She observes lions and cheetahs and tries to identify them, she sets up camera traps, she analyzes data, and she writes grant applications. She also gives talks and enjoys meeting with local villagers.
>
> Amy is good at working with big cats, and when she was asked what inspired her to dedicate her life to them, she said: "There is something so magnificent about their power, beauty, and sheer wildness, and I think it would be terrible if these animals died out in the wild. I believe that we have a responsibility to make sure that human actions don't wipe them out, not only because they have a right to exist, but because I think that future generations should know and be able to experience the magnificence of these incredible wild animals."

E.   SCAN   Scan the article and underline the sentences that show Amy's experience working with animals.

F.   Scan the article again and list five things she does at her job.

1. _____

2. _____

3. _____

4. _____

5. _____

G.   Amy has her dream job. On a separate piece of paper, write a paragraph about your dream job. What skills do you need? What experience do you need? Why would you love this job so much?

On the Job

A zoo worker performs a dental procedure on a hippo.

UNIT OUTCOMES

- Compare employee behavior and attitudes
- Interpret a pay stub
- Analyze benefit information
- Identify safe workplace behavior
- Communicate at work

Look at the photo and answer the questions.

1. What words would you use to describe the zoo worker?

2. What safety hazards do you think the zoo worker has to consider?

LESSON ❶ Attitudes at work

GOAL ▪ Compare employee behavior and attitudes

🎧
CD 1
TR 18
A. Listen to two employees talk about their jobs. What does Leticia do? What does So do?

B. **COMPARE** With a partner, write examples of the two employees' behavior in the table.

Leticia	So
comes to work on time	

C. **ANALYZE** In your opinion, who is the better employee? Why? Can you think of other examples of good and bad employee behavior? Add them to the table.

D. **Read the conversation. Look at the words in *italics*. Which are possessive adjectives and which are possessive pronouns?**

Ellen: *My* boss is quite demanding and she always wants *her* reports on time.

Leticia: *Your* manager is more demanding than *mine*.

Ellen: Yes, but *yours* is less friendly.

E. **Study the chart. Which possessive pronouns have an *-s* at the end? Which possessive adjectives and possessive pronouns are the same?**

Possessive Adjectives and Possessive Pronouns		
Possessive adjectives	**Rule**	**Example sentence**
my, your, his, her, our, their	Possessive adjectives show possession of an object and come before the noun.	This is *her* office.
Possessive pronouns	**Rule**	**Example sentence**
mine, yours, his, hers, ours, theirs	Possessive pronouns show possession of an object and act as a noun.	This office is *hers*.

F. **Underline the possessive adjective in each sentence. Circle the possessive pronoun.**

1. <u>My</u> sister's manager is generous, but <u>my</u> manager is more generous than (hers.)

2. Their job is boring, but our job is more boring than theirs.

3. My husband gets a good salary. His salary is better than mine.

4. My brother says his coworkers are friendly, but my coworkers are friendlier than his.

5. I like her manager, but mine is much more easygoing.

6. His office is clean, but ours is bigger.

G. Circle the correct word in each sentence.

1. She keeps (**her**/ hers) work space very clean.

2. She never eats at (her / hers) desk, but they always eat at (they / theirs).

3. That office is (you / yours).

4. (Theirs / Their) company has more employees than his.

5. That's (your / yours) book. Where is (my / mine)?

6. We will give you (our / ours) proposal so you can compare it with (your / yours).

H. Read the conversation between Leticia and Ellen.

Leticia: I think an ideal manager should be demanding.
Ellen: I agree. A manager shouldn't be too easygoing.

I.   ANALYZE What is an ideal manager like? What are ideal coworkers like? Use the adjectives from the box and have a conversation with your partner. Can you think of more adjectives?

friendly	courteous	funny	serious	demanding	respectful
strict	quiet	interesting	ambitious	hardworking	patient

J.   In a small group, talk about your current job or previous jobs. Using possessive pronouns write five sentences describing the experiences of your group members.

1. Anita has a friendly manager, but Jun's manager is friendlier than hers.

2. _____

3. _____

4. _____

5. _____

6. _____

LESSON **2** It's pay day!

A. Discuss the following vocabulary with your classmates and teacher.

year-to-date	marital status	rate of pay
earnings	Medicare	social security
federal tax	net pay	state disability
gross pay	payroll begin/end dates	tax deductions
401K	pre-tax deductions	

B. Look at Leticia's pay stub. Circle the vocabulary from the box in Exercise A.

<table>
<tr><td colspan="4" align="center">SECTION 1: PERSONAL DETAILS</td></tr>
<tr><td colspan="2">Employee Name: Leticia Rosales
Check Number: 0768
Social Security Number: 000-23-4567</td><td colspan="2">Marital Status: Single
Payroll Begin/End Dates:
5/14–5/27</td></tr>
<tr><td colspan="4" align="center">Hours and Earnings</td></tr>
<tr><td>Description</td><td>Rate of Pay</td><td>Hours/Units</td><td>Earnings</td></tr>
<tr><td>Hourly/Day/Monthly</td><td>14.75</td><td>80</td><td>1,180.00</td></tr>
</table>

<table>
<tr><td colspan="3" align="center">SECTION 2: TAX DEDUCTIONS</td></tr>
<tr><td>Tax Description</td><td>Current Amount</td><td>Calendar Year-to-Date</td></tr>
<tr><td>Federal Tax</td><td>102.78</td><td>205.56</td></tr>
<tr><td>State Tax</td><td>19.72</td><td>39.44</td></tr>
<tr><td>Social Security</td><td>10.68</td><td>21.36</td></tr>
<tr><td>Medicare</td><td>14.29</td><td>18.58</td></tr>
<tr><td>State Disability</td><td></td><td></td></tr>
</table>

<table>
<tr><td colspan="2" align="center">SECTION 3: PRE-TAX DEDUCTIONS</td></tr>
<tr><td align="center">Description</td><td align="center">Amount</td></tr>
<tr><td>401K</td><td>50.00</td></tr>
<tr><td>Current Total</td><td>50.00</td></tr>
<tr><td>Year-to-Date Total</td><td>100.00</td></tr>
</table>

<table>
<tr><td colspan="5" align="center">SECTION 4: TOTALS</td></tr>
<tr><td></td><td>Gross Pay</td><td>Pre-Tax Deductions</td><td>Tax Deductions</td><td>Net Pay</td></tr>
<tr><td>Current</td><td>1,180.00</td><td>50.00</td><td>147.47</td><td>982.53</td></tr>
</table>

C. **Where can you find the following information on Leticia's pay stub? Write the section number.**

Pay stub information	Section
weeks the paycheck covers	1
total amount she takes home	
information about retirement savings	
information about taxes	
hourly wage	

D. **Work with a partner to answer the questions about Leticia's pay stub. Take turns looking at the pay stub and asking questions.**

Student A: Is she married?
Student B: No.

1. Did she pay into social security this month? _____

   If so, how much? _____

2. Does she pay Medicare? _____

3. Does she pay state disability insurance? _____

4. How much federal tax has she paid this year? _____

5. How much money did she make this month before taxes? _____

6. How much state tax did she pay this month? _____

7. What does she get paid per hour? _____

8. What is her social security number? _____

E. **Discuss the questions with a partner.**

1. Would you rather get paid every week, twice a month, or once a month? Why?

2. Would you rather get paid a salary or get paid hourly? Why?

F. Look at the sentences below. Complete So's pay stub.

SECTION 1: PERSONAL DETAILS			
Employee Name: So Tran **Check Number:** 0498 **Social Security Number:** _____		**Marital Status:** _____ **Payroll Begin/End Dates:** 9/01–9/15	
Hours and Earnings			
Description	**Rate of Pay**	**Hours/Units**	**Earnings**
Hourly/Day/Monthly	_____	_____	740.00

SECTION 2: TAX DEDUCTIONS		
Tax Description	**Current Amount**	**Year-to-Date**
Federal Tax	27.16	_____
State Tax	5.29	95.22
Social Security	_____	120.24
Medicare	_____	167.22
State Disability		

SECTION 3: PRE-TAX DEDUCTIONS	
Description	**Amount**
401K	_____
Current Total	25.00
Year-to-Date Total	450.00

SECTION 4: TOTALS				
	Gross Pay	**Pre-Tax Deductions**	**Tax Deductions**	**Net Pay**
Current	_____	25.00	48.42	_____

1. So paid $6.68 into social security this month. So far this year, he has paid $120.24.

2. So paid $9.29 into Medicare this month.

3. His social security number is 000-56-8976.

4. So is married.

5. He contributes $25.00 every month into his 401K.

6. He makes $9.25 an hour.

7. His gross pay was $740.00.

8. He worked 80 hours this pay period.

9. His year-to-date federal tax deductions are $488.88.

G. CALCULATE What is So's net pay? (*Hint:* Subtract his deductions from his gross pay.)

LESSON **3** What are the benefits?

GOAL ■ Analyze benefit information

A. Benefits are extra things that a company offers its employees in addition to a salary. Read the list. Check (✔) the ones given at your current or previous jobs. Add another benefit that you know.

☐ 401K   ☐ maternity leave

☐ bonus   ☐ medical leave

☐ dental insurance   ☐ overtime

☐ disability insurance   ☐ paid personal days

☐ family leave   ☐ paid sick days

☐ health insurance   ☐ paid vacation days

☐ daycare   ☐ _____

B. Listen to the career counselor talk about the benefits that three companies offer. Make notes in the table.

CD 1
TR 19

Company	Health/Dental insurance	Sick days	Vacation days	401K
Set-It-Up Technology	full medical and dental insurance			yes–$1 for every dollar you contribute
Machine Works				
Lino's Ristorante				yes–50¢ for every dollar you contribute

C. EVALUATE Which company would you rather work for? Why? Discuss your answer with a partner.

D. Read about the benefits offered by some local companies in a small town in Utah.

> ### Employment Monthly
> #### Your Source for Employment Information in Well Springs, Utah
>
> **First Marketing** offers medical benefits, including dental insurance, disability insurance, family leave, medical leave, and maternity leave to all full-time employees. You'll get paid for up to six sick or personal days you need to take. In addition to the great health benefits, you'll have the opportunity to contribute to a 401K as well as receive bonuses based on productivity at the end of the year. Most employees work full-time and receive time and a half for any overtime they work.
>
> **Quick Clean** is a large chain of cleaners and there are employment opportunities at local stores in your community. All full-time employees receive health insurance. You can pay extra for dental insurance, but Quick Clean offers medical and maternity leave. All employees receive a certain number of sick days as well as vacation days, based on how long they have been with the company. Quick Clean doesn't offer any bonuses or 401K plans, but they encourage their employees to meet with their financial planner to help plan for retirement.
>
> **Ernie's Electrical** offers medical, dental, maternity, disability, and family leave to all full- and part-time employees. They give all of their employees three weeks a year to do with as they please— they can be used as sick days, personal days, or vacation days. No employees work overtime at Ernie's Electrical, which helps cut down on costs, but everyone receives a holiday bonus.

E. **ANALYZE** Decide which company would be best for him or her.

1. Alicia is a young, hardworking student who can only work part-time. She needs benefits because she lives by herself and has no family in Utah.

_____

2. Lars needs full benefits and likes to work overtime to make as much money as possible. He already has a 401K from another company that he would like to transfer to his new company.

_____

3. The most important thing for Su is maternity benefits. She and her husband are ready to start their family, but she still needs to work. She doesn't need dental insurance because her husband's company covers her.

_____

F. Complete the statements with a word or phrase from Exercise A.

1. _____Disability insurance_____ is for those who get injured at work.

2. At times, employees need to take time to care for a sick family member. This is called
   _____.

3. Most companies are required to offer their employees _____ to take
   care of them and their families when they are sick.

4. Some companies offer a retirement plan called a _____.

5. When a company shares its profits with the employees, each employee gets a
   _____.

6. When a woman has a new baby, she is allowed to take _____.

7. When you take a day off to do something for yourself, it is called a _____.

8. Some companies pay _____ when you work more than forty hours
   a week, or on weekends and holidays.

**G. GENERATE In a group, imagine that you are starting a company. Decide what
benefits you will offer. Answer the questions.**

1. How many sick days will each employee receive? _____

2. How many personal days will you give each employee? _____

3. How many vacation days will each employee get? _____

4. How much will you pay employees for overtime work? _____

5. What other benefits will you offer your employees? List them below.

   _____

   _____

   _____

   _____

   _____

LESSON **4** Workplace safety

GOAL ■ Identify safe workplace behavior

A. Look at the pictures. What type of job does each person have? Who needs to consider health issues? Who needs to consider safety issues?

Minh

Arnie

Wassim

Robin

B. Write the name of the person who should wear the safety items.

1. a back support belt _____

2. safety goggles _____

3. earplugs _____

4. a hairnet _____

C. Ask your partner if he or she wears safety items at work.

D. Read the conversation between Arnie and his manager, Fred. Do you think Fred is right?

Fred: Arnie, why aren't you wearing a back support belt?

Arnie: Oh, I don't need one.

Fred: If you don't wear a belt, you might get hurt.

Arnie: I don't think so. I'm really careful.

Fred: I know, but you could hurt your back if you lift something that is too heavy.

Arnie: You're right. If I get hurt, I might miss work. I could lose a lot of money if I can't work.

Fred: Exactly. Let me get you a belt.

E. *Might* and *could* are modals. Underline the modals in the conversation in Exercise D. Circle the verb that comes after each modal. Then, study the chart below.

Modals: *Could* and *Might*			
Subject	**Modal**	**Verb**	**Example sentence**
I, You, He, She, It, We, They	could	fall	You could fall.
	might	miss	I might miss work.

The modals *could* and *might* are used interchangeably because they mean the same. We use them to say that there is a chance that something will happen in the future.

F. We also use *might* and *could* in conditional sentences with *if* when we are talking about possibilities. Complete the sentences.

1. If Arnie doesn't wear a back support belt, ___*he could get hurt*_____.

2. If Minh forgets to tie her hair back, _____.

3. José _____ if he doesn't wear a hard hat.

4. Wassim _____ if he doesn't wear safety goggles.

5. Robin _____ if he doesn't wear earplugs.

6. If Lilly doesn't buckle her seat belt, she _____.

G. Look at the safety hazards. What's wrong in each picture?

1.

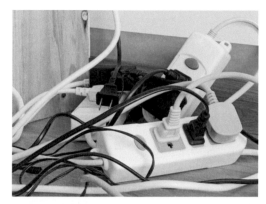

2.

3.

4.

H. **PREDICT** Write sentences about what *could/might* happen in the situations in Exercise G.

1. _____

_____

2. _____

_____

3. _____

_____

4. _____

_____

I. Work with a small group to make a list of safety rules for your classroom. Use *could* and *might*.

LESSON **5** Good job!

GOAL ■ Communicate at work

A. PREDICT Look at the picture. Is the manager criticizing or complimenting his employee? What do you think they are saying?

B. Identify the different types of communication. Write *compliment* or *criticism* next to each sentence.

1. Good job! _____*compliment*_____

2. You need to work a little faster. _____

3. You shouldn't wear that shirt to work. _____

4. That was an excellent presentation. _____

5. You are really friendly to the customers. _____

C. INTERPRET Are these people responding to criticism or a compliment? Write *compliment* or *criticism* next to each sentence. Then, listen and check your answers.

CD 1
TR 20

1. Thanks. I'm glad to hear it. _____

2. I'm sorry. I'll try to do better next time. _____

3. Thanks. _____

4. I'm sorry. I won't wear it again. _____

5. Thank you. I appreciate your telling me that. _____

D. **Use the sentences and responses in Exercises B and C to make conversations.**

Student A: Good job!
Student B: Thank you. I appreciate your telling me that.

E. **Compare the two conversations. Then, study the charts.**

Employee: Excuse me. Would you mind looking over this report for me before I send it out?

Manager: Yes, of course. That's no problem.

Susan: Could you give me a hand with this box?

Coworker: Sure, I'll be right over.

Polite Requests and Responses	
Would you mind helping me?	Polite and formal
Could you help me, *please?*	Polite and friendly
Can you give me a hand?	Polite and informal
Come here!	Very informal and impolite

When we speak to friends or colleagues, it is polite to be less formal. When we speak to a boss or a manager, it is polite to be more formal.

Agree	Refuse
Sure.	No. I'm really sorry.
That's fine.	I'm sorry, but I can't.
Of course.	I'd like to, but I can't because . . .
No problem.	
Certainly.	

RISING INTONATION FOR POLITE REQUESTS

Would you mind helping me?

Can you give me a hand?

Tone of Voice for Agreeing and Refusing

When you *agree* to something, your voice should sound *happy* and *upbeat*.

When you *refuse* something, you should sound *apologetic*.

F. Listen to these people talking to their bosses, coworkers, and employees. Are they being impolite or polite? Check (✔) the correct answer.

1. ☐ impolite ☐ polite   2. ☐ impolite ☐ polite

3. ☐ impolite ☐ polite   4. ☐ impolite ☐ polite

G. Complete the conversations with a partner. Then, practice your conversations and present them to the class.

Conversation 1

A: That was an excellent project you turned in.
B: _____
A: I'm going to share it with all the other employees.
B: _____

Conversation 2

A: Please don't be late to work anymore.
B: _____
A: It's really affecting your work.
B: _____

Conversation 3

A: _____
B: Sure, I'd be happy to.
A: _____

Conversation 4

A: _____
B: _____
A: _____
B: _____

H. Work with a partner. Practice making and responding to polite requests, and complimenting and criticizing.

1. Your manager gave you a good employee review.

2. Ask your coworker to give you a ride home.

3. Your coworker is always late.

4. Ask your boss to help you check some accounts.

Before You Watch

A. Look at the picture and answer the questions.

1. What is the relationship between Mr. Patel and Hector and Mateo?

2. What is Mr. Patel giving to Hector and Mateo?

While You Watch

B. ▶ Watch the video and complete the dialog.

Mateo: Well, these are all your deductions. Let me explain it this way. Let's say this is your check. At least ten percent goes to taxes. You pay about $50 for health (1) _____insurance_____, right?

Hector: And another $50 goes into my (2) _____.

Mateo: That's good. That's another (3) _____. Anything else?

Hector: Well, there's (4) _____, dental insurance, and transportation. Mr. Patel pays for part of my bus pass. That comes out of my check, too.

Mateo: This is what's left of your check. As you can see, almost one-third of your check is (5) _____. Surprising, isn't it?

Check Your Understanding

C. Write *T* for true and *F* for false.

1. Mr. Patel gives Hector and Mateo their paychecks every Thursday. _____

2. Hector pays about $50 in health insurance each week. _____

3. Mateo pays $50 into his 401K every week. _____

4. Hector has dental insurance, but Mateo doesn't. _____

5. Mr. Patel gives a bonus at the end of the year. _____

Review

Learner Log

I can compare employee behavior and attitudes.   I can analyze benefit information.
■ Yes ■ No ■ Maybe   ■ Yes ■ No ■ Maybe

A. **Work with a partner. Imagine that you need to hire several new employees for your business. Use the vocabulary from the box to talk about the qualities you are looking for.**

friendly	courteous	funny	serious	demanding	respectful
strict	quiet	interesting	ambitious	hardworking	patient

Student A: I think an ideal employee should be serious.
Student B: I agree. Good employees shouldn't be lazy.

B. **Circle the correct word in each sentence.**

1. Have you seen (my / mine) new pen?

2. (They / Their) cafeteria has delicious food, but (our / ours) is awful.

3. Can I use (your / yours) stapler? I can't find (my / mine.)

4. (Our / Ours) salary is low, but we get lots of tips.

5. (My / Mine) benefits are really good, but (her / hers) are better.

C. **Match the description to the benefit.**

_____ 1. 401K   a. for work injuries

_____ 2. bonus   b. a day off to do something for yourself

_____ 3. disability insurance   c. time off to have a baby

_____ 4. family medical leave   d. retirement savings

_____ 5. maternity leave   e. a day off if you are sick

_____ 6. personal day   f. when a company shares its profits

_____ 7. sick day   g. time off to care for a sick family member

D. Skim Ali's pay stub and answer the questions below.

SECTION 1: PERSONAL DETAILS	
Employee Name: Ali Ramsey **Check Number:** 89765 **SS Number:** 000-89-2524	**Marital Status:** Single **Payroll Begin/End Dates:** 8/01–8/15

Hours and Earnings			
Description	**Rate of Pay**	**Hours/Units**	**Earnings**
Hourly/Day/Monthly	11.75	56	658.00

SECTION 2: TAX DEDUCTIONS		
Tax Description	**Current Amount**	**Year-to-Date**
Federal Tax	17.65	141.20
State Tax	6.75	54.00
Social Security	5.23	41.84
Medicare	3.26	26.08
State Disability	4.25	34.00

SECTION 3: PRE-TAX DEDUCTIONS	
Description	**Amount**
401K	100.00
Current Total	100.00
Year-to-Date Total	800.00

SECTION 4: TOTALS				
	Gross Pay	**Pre-Tax Deductions**	**Tax Deductions**	**Net Pay**
Current	658.00	100.00	37.14	520.86

1. Did Ali pay into social security this month? _____

   If so, how much? _____

2. Does Ali pay Medicare? _____

3. Does he pay state disability insurance? _____

4. How many hours did he work during this two-week pay period? _____

5. How much federal tax has Ali paid this year? _____

6. Does he contribute any money to a retirement account? _____

   If so, how much? _____

7. How much money did he make this month after taxes? _____

8. How much money did he make this month before taxes? _____

9. How much state tax did he pay this month? _____

10. What does he get paid per hour? _____

E. Complete the following conditional sentences about work situations with *might* or *could*.

1. If you don't mop the wet floor, _____.

2. If the truck driver drives too fast, _____.

3. If those construction workers don't wear earplugs, _____.

4. If the gardener doesn't wear gloves, _____.

F. Work with a partner to match the conversations. Practice the conversations with a partner.

1. Your report was excellent!

2. I noticed you were late again today.

3. Can you work a little faster?

4. You finished that project so quickly!

a. I'm so sorry. I've been having car troubles.

b. It was really interesting to work on so I couldn't stop!

c. Thank you. I worked really hard on it.

d. Yes, I can.

G. Work with a partner. Practice making and responding to polite requests using the situations below.

1. Ask your coworker to let you use her computer.

2. Ask your employee to send a fax.

3. Ask your coworker to help you lift a heavy box.

H. Use your dictionary to look up different word forms of vocabulary in this unit. Use the new word form in a sentence.

1. nouns: employee, employer   verb: _to employ_____

   Our company wants to employ people with good computer skills.

2. noun: promotion   verb: _____

   _____

3. verb: to retire   noun: _____

   _____

✔ # Create an employee handbook

With your team, you will create one section of an employee handbook. With your class, you will create a complete employee handbook.

1. **COLLABORATE** Form a team with four or five students. Choose a position for each member of your team.

Position	Job description	Student name
Student 1: Leader	Check that everyone speaks English and participates.	
Student 2: Secretary	Write information for the handbook.	
Student 3: Designer	Design brochure layout and add artwork.	
Students 4/5: Member(s)	Help secretary and designer with their work.	

2. With your class, look at the list below. Decide which part of the handbook each team will create.
   - Pay Stub Information
   - Benefits
   - Workplace Safety
   - Workplace Communications

3. Create the text for your section of the employee handbook.

4. Create artwork for your section of the employee handbook.

5. As a class, create a table of contents and a cover. Put your handbook together.

6. Display your handbook so that other classes can see it.

Extreme Photography

"Creating films and photographs through situations that few others could experience is my life's inspiration."
—Jimmy Chin

A. PREDICT Look at the photo and answer the questions.

1. What are the people doing?

2. Do you think it could be dangerous to be a photographer? Why or why not?

B. Skim the article in Exercise C. What is the main idea?

1. Jimmy Chin takes risks to take amazing photographs.

2. Jimmy Chin's goal is to snowboard down Mount Everest.

3. Jimmy Chin's photography of Asian countries has appeared in *National Geographic* magazine.

C. Read about Jimmy Chin.

Jimmy Chin is a serious and hardworking photographer and filmmaker who captures shots that no one else can. He follows mountain climbers, skiers, and other trailblazers on their most dangerous adventures and takes pictures of them. Some of Jimmy's photographs have appeared in *National Geographic* magazine and in advertisements for companies like The North Face. Some people think their jobs are demanding, but Jimmy's is more demanding than most. Sometimes, he has to put himself in danger just to capture the moment with his camera. If Jimmy didn't take risks, he might miss an opportunity to take an amazing photograph.

In addition to being a photographer, he is a professional climber and skier. He has organized and been the leader of many climbing and skiing expeditions to Argentina, India, South Africa, China, and Pakistan, just to name a few. In 2003, Jimmy followed Stephen Koch to the North Face of Mount Everest to document him snowboarding down the world's tallest mountain. In 2006, he returned to Everest where he climbed to the summit. He then skied down to shoot Kit DesLauriers's famous ski descent. He and his team have also climbed Shark's Fin on Mount Meru in the Himalayas.

Jimmy has received several awards for his work. He hopes that the images and films from his expeditions will help him reach a greater goal. "It's about sharing stories that inspire people, highlight the infinite human spirit, and open people's eyes to a different world," Jimmy explains. "Creating films and photographs through situations that few others could experience is my life's inspiration."

D. SCAN What do the words mean? Scan the reading passage and match.

1. capture   a. never ending

2. document   b. motivate

3. boundaries   c. take a photo

4. attempt   d. a limit of activity

5. inspire   e. make a record of something

6. infinite   f. try something

E. It is important that Jimmy stays safe when he is working. Write two conditional sentences using *could* or *might* about possibilities.

1. _____

_____

2. _____

_____

Citizens and Community

A bridal party poses for a photo in a city neighborhood.

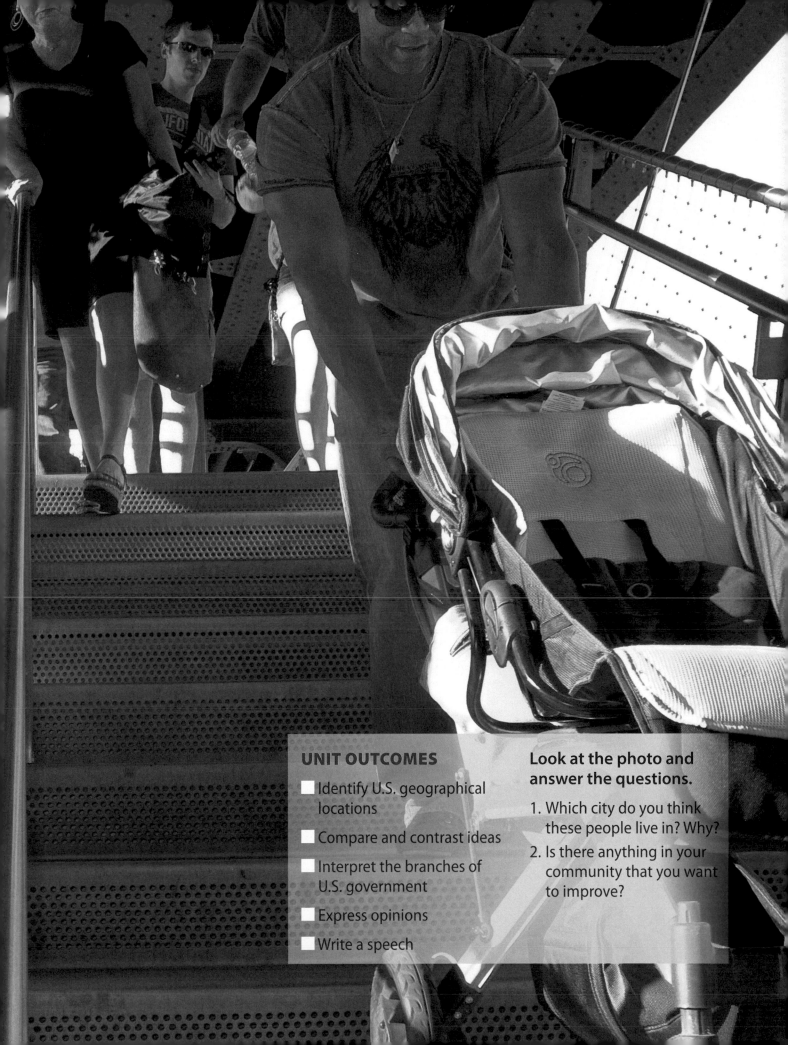

UNIT OUTCOMES

- Identify U.S. geographical locations
- Compare and contrast ideas
- Interpret the branches of U.S. government
- Express opinions
- Write a speech

Look at the photo and answer the questions.

1. Which city do you think these people live in? Why?
2. Is there anything in your community that you want to improve?

A. **LOCATE** Look at the map of the United States. Write the names of the cities in the spaces provided.

| Philadelphia | Los Angeles | Jamestown | New York | San Francisco | Houston |

B. Look at the map again. Write the names of any other cities you know in the United States.

_____

_____

_____

_____

_____

_____

_____

C. Read each state abbreviation and write the full state name. Ask a classmate or your teacher if you need help.

AL	Alabama	MT	_____
AK	_____	NE	Nebraska
AZ	_____	NV	_____
AR	Arkansas	NH	New Hampshire
CA	_____	NM	_____
CO	_____	NJ	_____
CT	Connecticut	NY	_____
DE	Delaware	NC	North Carolina
FL	_____	ND	North Dakota
GA	_____	OH	_____
HI	_____	OK	Oklahoma
ID	_____	OR	_____
IL	Illinois	PA	_____
IN	Indiana	RI	Rhode Island
IA	_____	SC	_____
KS	_____	SD	_____
KY	Kentucky	TN	Tennessee
LA	_____	TX	_____
ME	_____	UT	_____
MD	Maryland	VT	_____
MA	_____	VA	Virginia
MI	Michigan	WA	Washington
MN	_____	WV	_____
MS	Mississippi	WI	_____
MO	Missouri	WY	Wyoming

NOTE
Washington, D.C. is not a state.

D. **DETERMINE** Ask your partner about the states he or she has visited. Who has visited the most states?

E. Look at the pictures of popular tourist attractions in the United States. What are they? Where are they located?

F. Listen to the lecture on notable cities in the United States. Match the city with the correct information. Review the vocabulary before your start.

CD 1
TR 22

1. __g__ where the federal government is located   a. Houston, TX

2. _____ home of the Statue of Liberty   b. Jamestown, VA

3. _____ a major port for the Pacific Ocean   c. Los Angeles, CA

4. _____ an English colony named after an English king   d. New York, NY

5. _____ where the Declaration of Independence was written e. Philadelphia, PA

6. _____ the film capital of the world   f. San Francisco, CA

7. _____ a major oil producer   g. Washington, D.C.

8. _____ where Disney World is located   h. Orlando, FL

G. What else do you know about the cities listed in Exercise F? Discuss your ideas with your classmates and teacher.

H. Look at your list of cities in Exercise B. What are they known for? Include your own city or the city nearest you.

_____

_____

_____

_____

LESSON ② Which party?

GOAL ■ Compare and contrast ideas

A. The mayor is the leader of local government in most cities and towns in the United States. Do you know who your mayor is?

B. Imagine that you are getting ready to vote for a new mayor of your city. Two candidates gave speeches about what is important to them. Read their different points of view.

Kim Vo wants to . . .	Dawson Brooks wants to . . .
• build more parks.	• build more highways.
• lower class sizes in elementary schools.	• increase the number of teachers per classroom.
• lower the tuition at city colleges for immigrant students.	• raise the tuition at city colleges for immigrant students.
• spend tax dollars on wider sidewalks in neighborhoods.	• spend tax dollars to improve library facilities.
• increase the number of police officers who patrol the streets.	• spend money to retrain current police officers.
• offer job training programs for homeless people.	• offer incentives for individuals to start their own businesses.

C. With a partner, compare the two candidates using *but* and *however*.

Student A: Kim Vo wants to build more parks, **but** Dawson Brooks wants to build more highways.

Student B: Dawson Brooks wants to build more highways; **however**, Kim Vo wants to build more parks.

D. COMPARE Write two sentences comparing Kim Vo and Dawson Brooks using *but* or *however*.

1. _____

_____

2. _____

_____

E. EXPLAIN Which candidate would you vote for? Why? Write a paragraph on a separate piece of paper.

F. **FIND OUT** Ask your classmates about their feelings on the topics below. Think of your own topic for the last question.

Name	Topic	Agree	Disagree
Enrico	increasing the number of students in our class	✓	
Liz			✓

Name	Topic	Agree	Disagree
	building more schools in our community		

Name	Topic	Agree	Disagree
	providing bilingual education for children		

Name	Topic	Agree	Disagree

G. Study the chart with your classmates and teacher.

Comparing and Contrasting Ideas

If two people share the same opinion, use *both* and *and* or *neither* and *nor*.

Both Enrico *and* Liz	want to increase the number of students in our class.
Neither Enrico *nor* Liz	wants to increase the number of students in our class.

If two people don't share the same opinion, use *but* or *however*.

Enrico agrees with bilingual education,	*but* Liz doesn't.
Ali doesn't agree with bilingual education;	*however*, Suzana does.

Punctuation note: Use a semicolon (;) before and a comma (,) after *however*.

H. Complete each sentence with *both, and, neither, nor, but,* or *however.*

1. Neither Alicia _____ Hoa wants the city to build a school instead of a park.

2. _____ Kim and Su want to increase the number of hours that our class meets.

3. Jeeva thinks ESL students should be in class with native English speakers;

   _____, Adam thinks they should have their own class.

4. Bruno believes all children should study a second language, _____ Liza thinks children should learn only their native language.

5. _____ Lim nor Jeremy wants more homework.

6. Both Elizabeth _____ Parker want to do more writing in class.

I. COMPARE Look back at the information you collected on your classmates in Exercise F. Write sentences comparing their ideas.

1. _____

   _____

   _____

2. _____

   _____

   _____

3. _____

   _____

   _____

4. _____

   _____

   _____

LESSON **3** U.S. government

GOAL ■ Interpret the branches of U.S. government

A. **Look at the three branches that make up the U.S. government. What do you know about them?**

Executive

Legislative

Judicial

B. **DETERMINE** Read about the U.S. government. Then, answer the questions after each section.

> **The U.S. Government**
>
> The U.S. government has three branches—the executive branch, the legislative branch, and the judicial branch. The government was set up this way so no one person would have too much power. With three branches, each branch balances out the others.
>
> **The Executive Branch**
>
> The executive branch consists of the president, the vice president, and the cabinet. The president is the leader of the country and of the executive branch. He or she can sign new laws, prepare the budget, and command the military. The vice president helps the president and is the leader of the Senate. Both the president and the vice president serve for four years and can be reelected only once. The president's cabinet is a group of experts who advise the president. The president chooses his cabinet members. They include the Secretary of State, the Secretary of Defense, and the Secretary of Education.

1. What does the president do? _____

2. What does the vice president do? _____

3. How long do the president and vice president serve? _____

4. What does the cabinet do? _____

5. Are cabinet members elected? _____

The Legislative Branch

The legislative branch, also known as Congress, makes the laws for the United States. Congress has the power to declare war, collect taxes, borrow money, control immigration, set up a judicial and postal system, and the most important power, to make laws.

This branch has the greatest connection to the people of the United States because this branch represents citizens. Congress has two parts—the House of Representatives and the Senate. The House of Representatives has 435 state representatives. Each state gets a certain number of representatives based on its population. Each representative serves for two years and can be reelected. The Senate has 100 senators, two from each of the 50 states. Senators serve for six years and can also be reelected.

1. What is another name for the legislative branch? _____

2. What does this branch do? _____

3. What are the two parts of this branch called? _____

4. How many representatives are in the House? _____

5. What determines the number of representatives each state gets? _____

6. How long do representatives serve? _____

7. How many senators does each state have? _____

8. How long do senators serve? _____

The Judicial Branch

The third branch of the U.S. government is the judicial branch, which includes the Supreme Court and the federal courts. The job of the courts is to interpret the laws made by the legislative branch. The Supreme Court is the highest court in the United States and has nine judges called *justices*. The justices listen to cases and make judgments based on the Constitution and the laws of the United States. The president and Congress choose the justices of the Supreme Court.

1. What is the role of the judicial branch? _____

2. What is the highest court in the United States? _____

3. How does a person become a judge on the Supreme Court? _____

_____

C. Most cities have government officials who are elected to help run the city. Listen to the following people talk about their jobs and fill in the table with their duties.

Official	Duties
Tax assessor	1. helps county set tax rates 2. decides on the value of property
City clerk	1. 2.
City council member	1. 2.
Superintendent of schools	1. 2.
Mayor	1. 2.

D. **EVALUATE** Discuss the positions in the table above with a group. Which position would you most like to have? Why? Which one would you least like to have? Why? Write a paragraph below.

_____

_____

_____

_____

_____

_____

_____

_____

_____

GOAL ▪ Express opinions

A. **Cherie lives in a small town in California, but it's not as nice as it used to be. Read about the problems in Cherie's community.**

My name is Cherie. I live in a small community called Rosshaven in California. I moved here about ten years ago with my family because we wanted to live in a nice, safe community, but many things have happened in the past ten years.

First of all, the neighborhood schools are overcrowded. Because our school system is so good, many families from outside neighborhoods send their kids to our schools. There are over 35 students in each classroom.

Another problem is that there are many homeless people on our streets. It sometimes makes me nervous to have my kids walking home by themselves. I wish they could take a bus, but that's another problem. We don't have any public transportation here. When Rosshaven was first built, many wealthy people moved here. They all had cars, so there was no need for public transportation, but now things have changed. I think it's time for me to go to a city council meeting to see what I can do for our community.

B. **Cherie talks about three different problems. List them below.**

1. _____

2. _____

3. _____

C. GENERATE With a group, discuss possible solutions to each problem in Cherie's community. Write your ideas below. Report your answers to the class.

Problem	Possible solutions
	1. 2.
	1. 2.
	1. 2.

D. Rosshaven is a nice place to live, but like every community, it has some problems. Match each problem with a possible solution. Then, compare answers with a partner and say if you agree or disagree with each solution.

_____ 1. Visitors park in resident parking spaces.

_____ 2. People don't clean up after their pets.

_____ 3. Teenagers are out late at night getting into trouble.

_____ 4. The parks are not maintained.

a. Set a curfew for teenagers.

b. Fine people who don't clean up after their pets.

c. Give tickets to visitors who park in resident spaces.

d. Raise taxes to help with recreation improvements.

E. We use *should* to give a strong suggestion. Study the chart below with your teacher.

Modal *Should*			
Subject	**Modal**	**Base verb**	
The city council	*should*	set	a curfew for teenagers.
People	*should*	clean up	after their pets.

F. With your group, use *should* to talk about the solutions you wrote in Exercise C.

G. FORMULATE In a group, form a city council. Decide how you will solve the following problems and present your ideas to the class. The class will vote on which group would be the best city council.

1. There are no sidewalks on the busy streets in our town, and it is very dangerous. Many people get hurt because they walk too close to the cars. There is no space on the street to build sidewalks. What should we do to solve this problem?

    _____

    _____

    _____

    _____

2. The house prices are going up in our community. It's difficult to find affordable rent and almost impossible to buy a house. Many people are moving away from the community to find cheaper housing. The community wants to maintain diversity, but only the very wealthy can afford to stay. What should we do about the housing costs?

    _____

    _____

    _____

    _____

3. The town's river was very dirty, but groups of citizens did a lot to clean it up. We want to increase taxes so we can build a new park along the river, but the growing town needs a new supermarket and more office space, too. Is there a way to make everyone happy?

    _____

    _____

    _____

    _____

LESSON (5) If I were president

GOAL ■ Write a speech

A. Rosario's teacher asked her to write a paragraph about what she would do if she became president of the United States. Read what she wrote below.

> If I were president, nobody would be poor or homeless. Personally,
>
> I think if people had more money, they wouldn't commit crimes. In my opinion,
>
> we shouldn't spend so much money on the military. If scientists didn't have
>
> to build weapons, they would have more time to study other things.
>
> Maybe they would find a cure for cancer. I think that I'd be a great
>
> president!

B. Study these expressions with your classmates and teacher. Underline the ones Rosario used in her paragraph above.

In my opinion, …	I believe that …
As I see it, …	I think that …
Personally, I think …	I feel that …

C. **PLAN** On a separate piece of paper, write your opinion about the topics. Use the expressions from Exercise B.

1. the environment _I think we should be more concerned about the environment._

2. homeless people _____

3. homework _____

4. public transportation in my city _____

5. free English classes _____

D. Study the chart with your classmates and teacher.

Contrary-to-Fact Conditional Statements						
If	**Subject**	**Past tense verb (have) + noun**	**Subject**	**Modal**	**Base verb + noun**	**Example sentence**
If	I, you, he, she, we, they	had more money	I, you, he, she, we, they	would could	buy a house	If I had more money, I would buy a house.
If	I, you, he, she, we, they	didn't have the flu	I, you, he, she, we, they	would could	go to work	If he didn't have the flu, he could go to work.
If	**Subject**	**Past tense verb (be) + noun**	**Subject**	**Modal**	**Base verb + noun**	**Example sentence**
If	I, you, he, she, we, they	were president	I, you, he, she, we, they	would could	I would spend	If I were president, I would spend more money on education.
If	I, you, he, she, we, they	weren't so tired	I, you, he, she, we, they	would could	come to the movies	If they weren't so tired, they would come to the movies.

Contrary-to-fact (or unreal) conditional statements are sentences that are not true and that the speaker thinks will probably never be true.

Note: In written English, we use *were* instead of *was* in contrary-to-fact statements, but in spoken English, we often use *was* with the following subjects: I, he, and she.

E. Complete the sentences below with the correct form of the verbs in parentheses.

1. I ___would give___ (give) money to the homeless if ___I were___ (be) president.

2. If people _____ (have) more money, they _____ (be) happier.

3. If the president _____ (spend) more on health, scientists _____ (discover) a cure for cancer.

4. If our classes _____ (be) larger, the teacher _____ (not have) much time for each student.

5. Maria _____ (go) to medical school if she _____ (be) younger.

F. Look at the list of city officials on page 194. On a piece of paper, write a conditional statement for each official. Then, share your statements with a partner.

EXAMPLE: If I were the tax assessor, I would lower taxes.

G. **What would you do if you were president? Talk about the things you would like to change.**

Student A: What would you do if you were president?
Student B: Let's see. I think we need to improve our schools.
Student A: How would you do that?
Student B: I would pay teachers more. I would spend money on things like computers.

H. **Think about the following topics. What would you do if you were president? Write your ideas.**

Topic	My ideas
eliminating the death penalty	
raising the retirement age to 70	
raising the cost of gasoline so people would drive less	
smoking in public places	
raising the minimum wage	
building casinos to raise money for schools	

I. **VISUALIZE** Using the ideas you wrote above, write a paragraph about what you would do if you were president. Use Rosario's paragraph in Exercise A as an example. Then, share your paragraph with the class. Who would the class elect to be president?

_____

_____

_____

_____

_____

_____

LIFESKILLS ▶ Let's get ready to play

Before You Watch

A. **Look at the picture and answer the questions.**

1. What are Hector, Naomi, and Mateo doing?

2. What do you think Hector is asking Mateo and Naomi?

While You Watch

B. ▶ **Watch the video and complete the dialog.**

Mateo: Well, let's start with (1) _____ *geography* _____ because that's my specialty.

Naomi: OK, here's the first question. Which state is in the center of the country:

(2) _____, Colorado, or Kansas?

Hector: I know—um, (3) _____?

Mateo: Colorado and Arizona are both in the Southwest. So it must be

(4) _____.

Naomi: How right you are, Mateo. Kansas is in the central United States. It's in a region called the (5) _____.

Check Your Understanding

C. **Write *T* for true and *F* for false.**

1. Mateo's specialty is history. _____

2. Colorado is in the center of the country. _____

3. New York City is the oldest city in the United States. _____

4. Naomi answered the second question correctly. _____

5. You have to be born in the United States to be president. _____

Review

A. Write the full name of each state next to its abbreviation. See how many you can remember before you look back at page 187.

1. NY _____

2. CA _____

3. WA _____

4. FL _____

5. TX _____

6. ME _____

7. IL _____

8. NV _____

9. HI _____

10. NJ _____

B. Read the table below. Write sentences using *both . . . and, neither . . . nor, but,* and *however.*

EXAMPLE: _Both Sophia and Jamal want to increase class size._

Name	Topic	Agree	Disagree
Sophia	increasing the number of students in our class	✓	
Jamal		✓	
Sophia	building more parks in the community		✓
Jamal		✓	
Sophia	hiring more police officers	✓	
Jamal			✓
Sophia	building more freeways		✓
Jamal			✓

1. _____

_____

2. _____

_____

3. _____

_____

Learner Log

I can interpret the branches of U.S. government. I can express opinions.
☐ Yes ☐ No ☐ Maybe   ☐ Yes ☐ No ☐ Maybe

C. Check (✓) the correct branch of government after each statement.

	Legislative	Executive	Judicial
1. listens to cases and makes judgments			
2. interprets the laws			
3. signs new laws			
4. includes the president's cabinet			
5. includes the House of Representatives			
6. makes laws			
7. can control immigration			
8. commands the military			
9. includes the Congress			
10. chooses the justices of the Supreme Court			

D. Look at the community problems below. Write a solution for each problem using *should*.

1. **Problem:** traffic on the freeways

   Solution: The city should build more carpool lanes.

2. **Problem:** smoking in parks near playgrounds

   Solution: _____

3. **Problem:** cars driving too fast in residential areas

   Solution: _____

4. **Problem:** potholes

   Solution: _____

5. **Problem:** high crime rates

   Solution: _____

E. Complete these contrary-to-fact conditionals with the correct form of the verbs in parentheses.

1. I _____ (work) faster if I _____ (have) a computer.

2. If she _____ (live) in Italy, she _____ (eat) pizza every day.

3. If it _____ (stop) raining, we _____ (play) outside.

4. If the town _____ (buy) more land, we _____ (build) schools.

F. What would you do if you were mayor of your city? Write a paragraph stating your opinions about various local issues. Then, say what you would do if you were mayor.

In my opinion, the public transportation system in this town is very poor. The buses are always

late because there is too much traffic. If I were mayor, I would build a subway system and . . .

_____

_____

_____

_____

_____

G. Practice writing an entry in a vocabulary book. Start a vocabulary notebook of your own. Add any new words you have learned inside or outside of class.

Word: legislature

Part of speech: noun

Definition: a branch of the U.S. government that passes laws

Related word(s): legislation *(n)*, legislate *(v)*

Example sentence: The <u>legislature</u> passed a new law on gasoline taxes.

✔ **Run for mayor**

With your team, you will run a mayoral campaign. You will write a list of community problems and your solutions and create a flyer that will help you gain votes. You will also write a speech that you would give if you were elected mayor.

1. **COLLABORATE** Form a team with four or five students. Choose a position for each member of your team.

Position	Job description	Student name
Student 1: Leader	Check that everyone speaks English. Check that everyone participates.	
Student 2: Secretary	Write down the community problems, possible solutions, and the speech.	
Student 3: Designer	Create the flyer.	
Students 4/5: Member(s)	Help the secretary and the designer with their work.	

2. Imagine someone on your team is running for mayor of your city. Answer the following questions:

   Why would you want to be mayor?

   Why would you be the best mayor?

3. Come up with a list of community problems and your solutions to those problems.

4. Create a flyer including all your information and any appropriate pictures or art.

5. Write a speech that you would give as mayor.

6. Present your flyer and speech to the class.

Thomas Menino was mayor of Boston from 1993 until 2014 and well-loved by the people in the city.

Saving Lives with Music

"I don't want to see anyone go through what I did because of unclean water."
—Feliciano dos Santos

A. **PREDICT** Look at the photo. What do you think Feliciano dos Santos does?

B. **SKIM** Skim the first sentence of each paragraph. What do you think Feliciano is doing to help his community?

Niassa Province is in the north.

C. **Read about Feliciano dos Santos.**

Feliciano dos Santos is a musician and an activist who writes songs to help fight disease. When Feliciano was a young boy, he got polio from the contaminated water in his village. The disease left him handicapped. "I don't want to see anyone else go through what I did because of unclean water," he says.

Feliciano has been focusing his efforts on Niassa Province in Mozambique, where he was born and still lives today. In his community, people don't live very long, over half of the people are poor, and most homes don't have electricity or running water. Feliciano believes the people in his village should know how to care for themselves. He says that people don't usually like to talk about sanitation and hygiene, but once you add music and rhythm, they don't mind singing and dancing about it. One of his biggest hits is called "Wash Your Hands."

Feliciano started a nongovernmental organization (NGO) that offers projects to improve people's health and bring people out of poverty. Neither he nor the people he works with want to see the people of Niassa province get sick. One project is to install pumps for clean water. Another is to bring supplies to sick and orphaned children. The NGO also supports HIV/AIDS education. "Even when the right HIV/AIDS medicine reaches our villages, people may swallow the pills with contaminated water. Until we address that, how can any other initiative be truly effective?"

If Feliciano had more money and resources, he would buy more medicine and try to help more people, but for now he will do everything he can to make sure young children don't get diseases from contaminated water.

D. **SCAN** **Scan the article for the words below. Write your own sentences with each word.**

1. contaminated adj. unclean, impure

_____

2. prevent v. to block, make impossible

_____

3. hygiene n. maintaining health

_____

4. orphan n. a child whose parents have died

_____

5. disease n. a sickness that is caused by infection or bad living conditions

_____

E. **VISUALIZE** **Imagine that you are Feliciano dos Santos and you are running for mayor. Write a speech talking about what you would change in Niassa Province and how.**

The Secrets of Living Longer

An elderly Japanese fisherman hauls in his fishing nets.

In Unit 5, you met National Geographic explorer Dan Buettner. You read about a group of people in Sardinia who have a high life expectancy. Along with photographer David McLain, Dan visited two other groups of people who live long lives: the residents of Okinawa, Japan, and Loma Linda, California. His research appeared in the *National Geographic* magazine and you can find out more on the National Geographic website.

Before You Watch

A. **Look at the words and their definitions. Fill in the blanks with the correct choices.**

longevity   long duration of a person's life
centenarian   person who lives to or over 100 years
sedentary   inactive; spending too much time seated
obesity   condition of being overweight
outlive   to live longer than another person

1. People who have a Mediterranean diet are known for their _____.

2. Schools are trying to solve the problem of _____ by offering healthy meals to students.

3. Any person who becomes a _____ in the United Kingdom receives a birthday message from the Queen.

4. Some people believe that the advances in technology mean people are living more _____ lifestyles than ever before.

5. In the United States, the average woman can _____ the average man by five years.

B. **Check (✓) the items that you think contribute to a healthy lifestyle. Look up any words you don't know.**

   ▢ lack of stress   ▢ low calorie intake
   ▢ strong connections to friends and family   ▢ obesity
   ▢ sedentary lifestyle   ▢ high alcohol intake
   ▢ locally sourced food   ▢ smoking
   ▢ fast food   ▢ rest
   ▢ active lifestyle   ▢ exercise
   ▢ positive outlook on life   ▢ routine

C. **You are going to watch a video. Look at the images and quotes below. What do you think this video will be about? Discuss with a partner.**

"What is **phenomenal** (great) about this region is that men are living just as long as women."

"He met an amazing woman who was over a hundred."

"Okinawa is losing its longevity **edge** (advantage)."

" … the Seventh Day Adventists … have a religion that reinforces positive, healthy behaviors."

Watch the video. Mark the items you see.

- family meal
- cell phones
- fast food
- natural medicine
- friends
- computer games
- dancing
- swimming
- smoking
- healthy food
- cycling
- acupuncture

After You Watch

A. The video mentions the factors that contribute to longevity in each culture. Check (✓) the items that correspond to each place. Some items may correspond to more than one place.

	Sardinia	Okinawa	Loma Linda
a positive outlook on life			
no drinking			
exercise			
active lifestyle			
lack of stress			
rest			
no smoking			
strong connection to family/friends			
low calorie intake			
locally sourced food			

B. Read the sentences. Circle *T* for true and *F* for false. Correct the false sentences in your notebook.

1. Sardinian men live longer because women make important decisions. T F

2. People live longer in Okinawa because they spend time alone. T F

3. All Seventh Day Adventists are vegetarians. T F

4. The culture of longevity is disappearing in Sardinia. T F

5. The people of Okinawa do not eat much food. T F

6. People in Loma Linda live ten years less than other Americans. T F

C. **Complete the sentences with the words below.**

| longevity | centenarian | sedentary | obesity | outlive |

1. The Seventh Day Adventists are the only group of people David visited who are not losing their _____ edge.

2. According to the video, Okinawa has the highest rate of _____ in Japan.

3. David met one _____ who had just renewed her driver's license.

4. Current Sardinians are leading a more _____ lifestyle that means they may not live as long as their grandparents.

5. Seventh Day Adventists _____ other Americans by about ten years.

D. **Which culture of longevity appeals to you the most? Why? Discuss with a partner.**

EXAMPLE: I like the Sardinian way because men live as long as women, and I'm a man!

E. **What about your own culture? Does it have anything in common with the cultures in the video? Write similarities and differences.**

Similarities   Differences

_____   _____

_____   _____

F. **Get together in a group of four. Explain to your group how your culture is similar and different from these three cultures of longevity.**

A Sardinian girl wears traditional dress.

STAND OUT VOCABULARY LIST

PRE-UNIT
Registration
date of birth 3
first name 3
last name 3
middle initial 3
occupation 3
Education
achieve 11
college 9
community college 9
elementary school 9
formatting 8
goal 6
graduate school 9
high school 9
indent 7
junior high school 9
kindergarten 9
middle school 9
paragraph margins 7
preschool 9
successful 7
university 9
vocational 9

UNIT 1
accomplish 27
balance 26
beneficial 24
benefits 27
concentrate 24
conclusion 21
distractions 24
frequency adverbs 15
goals 17
harmful 24
improve 24
obstacle 17
occupational 19
personal 19
routine 14
schedule 14
solution 18
study habits 23
support 21
task 27
time slot 27
topic 21

UNIT 2
ad 41
adjectives 45
advantages 48
advertisement 41
bank 38
car wash 38
cash 47
CD drive 44
check 47
comparative and
    superlative 45–46
comparison shopping 50
consumer 36
credit card 47
debit card 47
department store 38
disadvantages 48
discount 41
dry cleaners 38
expire 41
gas station 38
goods 38
grocery store 38
guarantee 41
hard drive 44
installation 41
irregular adjectives 45
jewelry store 38
keyboard 44
laundromat 38
memory 44
must 49
offer 41
percent off 41
pharmacy 38
post office 38
regular 41
sale 41
save 41
screen 44
sequence transitions 51
services 38
smart consumer 50
speed 44
tailor 38
touch pad 44
USB port 44
warranty 41

UNIT 3
air conditioning 65
arrange 68
balcony 62
baseline 68
cancel 68
carpeting 65
carport 62
charming 62
classified ad 62
condition 62
electrician 74
exterminator 74
fix 74
garage 65
graph 72
handyman 75
hookup 64
maintenance 71
mouse 75
plumber 74
pool 65
preferences 65
repairs 74
roaches 74
security guard 62
salary 71
tennis courts 65
therms 68
total 71
utility 68
yard 65

UNIT 4
ATM 89
branch 90
car registration 86
check out 90
circulation 90
class registration 86
deposit 95
direct deposit 102
dry cleaning 95
east 92
errands 95
far 93
fee 91
fine 90
librarian 90

lose 90
minimum daily balance 89
north 92
northeast 92
northwest 92
overdue 90
permit 91
reference 90
renewal 91
replacement 91
run 93
service fee 89
teller 102
transactions 89
south 92
southeast 92
southwest 92
unlimited 89
valid 91
west 92

UNIT 5
% daily value 124
aerobics 127
allergies 115
amount 124
backache 117
balance 131
calories 124
carbohydrate 124
cardiovascular 128
cause 121
cavities 121
cholesterol 124
cold 119
conditions 116
digestion 125
diseases 116
dizzy 119
effect 121
fat 124
grain 123
fiber 124
habit 120
headache 117
healthy weight 126
illness 119
liver 120
lungs 120

STAND OUT GRAMMAR REFERENCE

Comparatives				
	Adjective	**Comparative**	**Rule**	**Example sentence**
Short adjectives	cheap	cheaper	Add *-er* to the end of the adjective.	Your computer was *cheaper* than my computer.
Long adjectives	expensive	more expensive	Add *more* before the adjective.	The new computer was more *expensive* than the old one.
Irregular adjectives	good bad	better worse	These adjectives are irregular.	The computer at school is *better* than this one.

Remember to use *than* after a comparative adjective followed by a noun.

Superlatives				
	Adjective	**Superlative**	**Rule**	**Example sentence**
Short adjectives	cheap	the cheapest	Add *-est* to the end of the adjective.	Your computer is the *cheapest*.
Long adjectives	expensive	the most expensive	Add *most* before the adjective.	He bought *the most* expensive computer in the store.
Irregular adjectives	good bad	the best the worst	These adjectives are irregular.	The computers at school are *the best*.

Always use *the* before a superlative.

Must vs. *Have to*			
Subject	**Modal**	**Base verb**	
We	have to	save	money for vacation.
I	must	pay off	my credit card every month.

Comparatives Using Nouns	
Our new apartment has more *bedrooms* than our old one. Our old apartment had fewer bedrooms than our new one.	Use *more* or *fewer* to compare count nouns.
Rachel's apartment gets *more light* than Pablo's apartment. Pablo's apartment gets *less light* than Rachel's apartment.	Use *more* or *less* to compare noncount nouns.

Superlatives Using Nouns

Rachel's apartment has *the most bedrooms*. Phuong's apartment has *the fewest bedrooms*.	Use *the most* or *the fewest* for count nouns.
Rachel's apartment has *the most light*. Phuong's apartment has *the least light*.	Use *the most* or *the least* for non-count nouns.

Yes/No Questions and Answers with *Do*

Questions				Short answers
Do	Subject	Base verb	Example question	
do	I, you, we, they	have	Do they have a yard?	Yes, they do. / No, they don't.
does	he, she, it	want	Does she want air-conditioning?	Yes, she does. / No, she doesn't.

Information Questions

Question words	Example questions
How	*How* may I help you?
What	*What* is your current address?
When	*When* would you like your service turned off?

Past Continuous

Subject	*be*	Verb + *ing*	Example sentence
I, He, She, It	was	making	I was making breakfast.
You, We, They	were	studying	They were studying.

Use the past continuous to talk about things that started in the past and continued for a period of time.

Past Continuous Using *While*

Subject	*be*	Verb + *ing*	Example sentence
I, He, She, It	was	making	While I was making dinner, I saw a mouse.
You, We, They	were	studying	The electricity went out while we were studying.

To connect two events that happened in the past, use the past continuous with *while* for the longer event. Use the simple past for the shorter event.
Note: You can reverse the two clauses, but you need a comma if the *while* clause comes first.

Information Questions

Location	Where	is the bank?
	How far	is the school from here?
	What	is the address?
Time	When	does the library open?
	What time	does the restaurant close?
	How often	do the buses run?
Cost	How much	does it cost?

Adverbial Clauses with *Before, After* and *When*

EXAMPLE	RULE
After I returned the books, I stopped by the bank to make a deposit.	The action closest to *after* happened first. (First, she returned the books. Second, she went to the bank)
Before I went grocery shopping, I stopped by the cleaners to pick up some skirts.	The action closest to *before* happened second. (First, she went to the cleaners. Second, she went grocery shopping.)
When everyone left the house, I made my list of errands and off I went.	The action closest to *when* is completed and then next act begins. (First, everyone left. Second, she made her list.)
I went home **when** I finished shopping. **When** I finished shopping, I went home.	You can reverse the two clauses and the meaning stays the same. You need a comma if the adverbial clause goes first.

Present Perfect

Subject	*have*	Past participle		Time	Example sentence
I, You We, They	have	been	sick	since Tuesday	I *have been* sick since Tuesday.
She, He, It	has	had	a backache	for two weeks	She *has had* a backache for two weeks.

Use the present perfect for events starting in the past and continuing up to the present.

Future Conditional Statements

Cause: *If* + present tense	Effect: future tense
If you *are* very stressed,	you *will have* high blood pressure.
If you *don't get* enough calcium,	you *won't have* strong bones.

We can connect a cause and an effect by using a *future conditional* statement. The *if*-clause (or the *cause*) is in the present tense and the *effect* is in the future tense.

Effect: future tense	Cause: *if* + present tense
You *will have* high blood pressure	*if* you *are* very stressed.

You can reverse the clauses, but use a comma only when the *if*-clause comes first.

Infinitives and Gerunds
Infinitive = *to* + verb   Gerund = verb + *ing*

Verb	Infinitive or Gerund?	Example sentence	Other verbs that follow the same rule
want	infinitive	He wants *to get* a job.	plan, decide
enjoy	gerund	He enjoys *fixing* bicycles.	finish, give up
like	both	He likes *to talk*. He likes *talking*.	love, hate

Gerunds and Nouns after Prepositions

Subject	Verb	Adjective	Preposition	Gerund/Noun	Example sentence
I	am	good	at	calculating	I am good at *calculating*.
She	is	good	at	math	She is good at *math*.

A gerund or a noun follows an adjective + a preposition. Some other examples of adjectives + prepositions are *interested in, afraid of, tired of, bad at,* and *worried about*.

Would rather

Subject	*would rather*	Base form	*than*	Base form	Example sentence
I, You, She, He, It We, They	would ('d) rather	work alone	than	work with people	I would rather work alone than work with people.

Note: You can omit the second verb if it is the same as the first verb.
Example: I would rather work nights than (work) days.

Possessive Adjectives and Possessive Pronouns

Possessive adjectives	Rule	Example sentence
my, your, his, her, our, their	*Possessive adjectives* show possession of an object and come before the noun.	This is *her* office.
Possessive pronouns	**Rule**	**Example sentence**
mine, yours, his, hers, ours, theirs	*Possessive pronouns* show possession of an object and act as a noun.	This office is *hers*.

Modals: *Could* and *Might*

Subject	Modal	Verb	Example sentence
I, You, He, She, It, We, They	could	fall	You could fall.
	might	miss	I might miss work.

We use the modals *could* and *might* to say that there is a chance that something will happen in the future.

Comparing and Contrasting Ideas

If two people share the same opinion, use *both . . . and* or *neither . . . nor*.

Both	Enrico **and** Liz	<u>want</u> to increase the number of students in our class.
Neither	Suzanna **nor** Ali	<u>wants</u> to increase the number of students in our class.

If two people don't share the same opinion, use *but* or *however*.

Enrico agrees with bilingual education,	**but** Liz doesn't.
Ali doesn't agree with bilingual education;	**however,** Suzanna does.

Punctuation Note: Use a semicolon (;) before and a comma (,) after *however*.

Should

Subject	Modal	Base verb	
The city council	should	set	a curfew for teenagers.
People	should	clean up	after their pets.

Contrary-to-Fact Conditional Statements

if	Subject	Past tense verb	Subject	*Would*	Base verb	Example sentence
If	I, you, she, he, we, they	had didn't have	I	would wouldn't	buy	If I had more money, I would buy a new house
If	I, you, she, he, we, they	were was were't (wasn't)	I	would wouldn't	spend	If I were (was) president, I would spend more money on education.

Contrary-to-fact (or unreal) conditional statements are sentences that are not true and that the speaker thinks will probably never be true.

Note: In written English, we use *were* instead of *was* in contrary-to-fact conditionals, but in spoken English we often use *was*.

Stand Out 3 Irregular Verb List

The following verbs are used in *Stand Out 3* and have irregular past tense forms.

Base Form	Simple Past	Past Participle
be	was, were	been
become	became	become
break	broke	broken
build	built	built
buy	bought	bought
catch	caught	caught
choose	chose	chosen
come	came	come
do	did	done
drink	drank	drunk
drive	drove	driven
eat	ate	eaten
fall	fell	fallen
feel	felt	felt
fly	flew	flown
forget	forgot	forgotten
find	found	found
get	got	gotten
give	gave	given
go	went	gone
hang	hung	hanged/hung
have	had	had
hear	heard	heard
hold	held	held
hurt	hurt	hurt
keep	kept	kept
know	knew	known
learn	learned	learned/learnt
leave	left	left

Base Form	Simple Past	Past Participle
lend	lent	lent
lose	lost	lost
make	made	made
mean	meant	meant
meet	met	met
pay	paid	paid
put	put	put
read	read	read
ride	rode	ridden
run	ran	run
say	said	said
sell	sold	sold
shake	shook	shaken
show	showed	shown
sit	sat	sat
sleep	slept	slept
speak	spoke	spoken
spend	spent	spent
stand	stood	stood
take	took	taken
teach	taught	taught
tell	told	told
think	thought	thought
throw	threw	thrown
wake	woke	woken
wear	wore	worn
win	won	won
write	wrote	written

PHOTO CREDITS

Cover: Dimitri Otis/Getty Images; James Porter/Getty Images; Jay B Sauceda/Getty Images; Dear Blue/ Getty Images; Jade/Getty Images; Mark Edward Atkinson/Tracey Lee/ Getty Images; Seth Joel/Getty Images; Tripod/Getty Images; Portra Images/ Getty Images; Portra Images/Getty Images; LWA/Larry Williams/Getty Images; Hero Images/Getty Images

02 (tl) Portra Images/Getty Images, (tc) Portra Images/Getty Images, (tr) Mark Edward Atkinson/Tracey Lee/ Getty Images, (bl) Hero Images/ Getty Images, (bc) Jade/Getty Images (br) Seth Joel/Getty Images; **05** Helder Almeida/Shutterstock .com; **12–13** Paul Chesley/National Geographic Creative; **18** (cl) Pistolseven/Shutterstock.com, (bl) Dragon Images/Shutterstock. com, **21** Todd Heisler/The New York Times/Redux; **26** (b) IM_photo/ Shutterstock.com; **29** © Cengage Learning; **33** (b) Luciano Mortula/ Shutterstock.com; **34** Bobby Model/ National Geographic Creative; **36–37** Randy Olson/National Geographic Creative; **38** (cl) Ariadna de raad/Shutterstock.com; (cr) Timur Kulgarin/Shutterstock. com; **39** moodboard plus/Corbis; **41** (cl) ifong/Shutterstock.com, (cr) Bohbeh/Shutterstock.com, (bl) bergamont/Shutterstock.com, (br) Julian Rovagnati/Shutterstock .com; **43** (tl) Andrey_Popov/ Shutterstock.com, (tr) Milos Tasic/Getty Images; **44** (tl) Luis Louro/Shutterstock.com, (tr) Boonchuay1970/Shutterstock.com; **47** (tl) © Cengage Learning; **50** Tyler Olson/Shutterstock.com; **52** ifong/ Shutterstock.com; **53** © Cengage Learning; **54** (cl) zentilia/ Shutterstock.com, (cr) zentilia/

Shutterstock.com, **58** www .jamesperrin.com; **59** Mikhaylova Oxana/Shutterstock.com; **60–61** Tse Hon Ning/Getty Images; **69** Olivier Le Queinec/Shutterstock. com; **77** © Cengage Learning; **81** Pics-xl/Shutterstock.com; **82** Paul Colangelo/National Geographic Creative; **84–85** Rickett & Sones; **91** zerocreatives/Westend61/ Corbis; **95** Monkey Business Images/ Shutterstock.com; **101** © Cengage Learning; **105** Jeremy Reddington/ Shutterstock.com; **106** Kenneth Garrett/National Geographic Creative; **108** (t) Hatnim Lee/ National Geographic's Genographic Project; **110** (tl) National Geographic Society Genographic Project, (tr) National Geographic Society Genographic Project, (cl) National Geographic Society Genographic Project, (cr) National Geographic Society Genographic Project; **112–113** Robert Clark/ National Geographic Creative; **114** mooinblack/Shutterstock.com; **117** (cl) kurhan/Shutterstock.com, (c) Cessna152/Shutterstock.com, (cr) wavebreakmedia/Shutterstock .com, (bl) VGstockstudio/ Shutterstock.com, (bc) Image Point Fr/Shutterstock.com, (br) wavebreakmedia/Shutterstock .com; **121** hamdan/Shutterstock .com; **126** VGstockstudio/ Shutterstock.com, **127** (cr) William Perugini/Shutterstock.com, (cl) Dragon Images/Shutterstock .com; **129** © Cengage Learning; **133** Emmanuel R Lacoste/ Shutterstock.com; **134** (t) Richard Tsong-Taatarii/Corbis Wire/Corbis, (br) David McLain/Aurora Photos; **136–137** Al Seib/Getty Images; **138** (tl) StockLite/Shutterstock.com, (tr) Andrey_Popov/Shutterstock .com, (cl) Wavebreakmedia/

Shutterstock.com, (cr) Sergey Mironov/Shutterstock .com; **139** (cl) Wavebreakmedia/ Shutterstock.com, (c) Pressmaster/ Shutterstock.com, (c) Andrey Popov/Shutterstock.com, (cr) Dmitry Kalinovsky/Shutterstock.com, (bl) Alexander Raths/Shutterstock .com, (bc) Kinga/Shutterstock .com, (bc) Wavebreakmedia/ Shutterstock.com, (br) Stephen Coburn/Shutterstock.com; **142** Charles Gupton/Stock Boston; **151** (cl) auremar/Shutterstock.com, (bl) michaeljung/Shutterstock .com; **153** © Cengage Learning, **158** Anne Schimidt-Kuentzel; **160–161** Raul Arboleda/Getty Images; **162** (tl) Tiffany Schoepp/ Jupiter Images, (tr) Alexander Hogan/Alamy; **173** (tl) Barnaby Chambers/Shutterstock.com, (tr) Stephen Barnes/Security/ Alamy, (cl) iStock/Getty Images Plus/Getty Images, (cr) Flavio Knüsel/EyeEm/ Getty Images; **174** Jon Feingersh/ Getty Images; **177** © Cengage Learning; **182** Camp4 Collective; **184–185** Diane Cook/Len Jenshel/National Geographic Creative; **188** (tl) Nickolay Stanev/ Shutterstock.com, (tc) Matej Hudovernik/Shutterstock.com, (tr) f11photo/Shutterstock.com; **192** (tl) tigerbarb/Shutterstock .com, (tc) J Main/Shutterstock.com, (tr) Joe Ravi/Shutterstock.com; **201** © Cengage Learning; **205** Rick Nohl/Corbis News/Corbis; **206** (t) © Goldman Environmental Prize; (br) Volina/Shutterstock.com; **208** David McLain/Aurora Photo; **209** (bl) © National Geographic Learning, (bc) © National Geographic Learning, (bc) © National Geographic Learning, (br) © National Geographic Learning; **211** Maxvan23/Shutterstock.com.

STAND OUT SKILLS INDEX

ACADEMIC SKILLS

Charts, tables, and maps, 19, 25, 28, 39, 43, 45, 46, 48, 63, 66, 72, 75, 87, 89, 91, 92, 94, 103, 118, 121, 142, 143, 151, 152, 163, 168, 186, 190, 199, 202

Critical thinking

analyze, 7, 14, 20, 22, 59, 76, 83, 96, 120, 124, 135, 138, 148, 162, 164, 169

apply, 5, 19, 40, 43, 46, 49, 52, 73, 76, 88, 143

calculate, 167

classify, 19, 38

collaborate, 33, 57, 81, 105, 133, 157, 181, 205

compare, 8, 10, 23, 25, 48, 63, 189, 191

compose, 8, 11, 100, 162

construct, 66

create, 16, 91, 146

decide, 89

demonstrate, 86, 93

determine, 74, 76, 88, 146, 147, 151, 187, 192

describe, 44, 92, 119

discuss, 27

evaluate, 42, 45, 70, 120, 124, 141, 143, 146, 168, 194

explain, 39, 62, 128, 150, 189

find out, 3, 41, 190

formulate, 99, 197

generate, 170, 196

identify, 18, 44, 47, 140

illustrate, 72–73

infer, 90

interpret, 15, 24, 41, 65, 68, 69, 71, 145, 174

justify, 43

locate, 186

plan, 125, 198

predict, 9, 34, 58, 82, 106, 134, 158, 173, 174, 182, 206

prepare, 152

put in order, 50, 95, 98

recall, 114

reflect, 28

restate, 6

scan, 64, 183, 159, 207

skim, 158, 206

suggest, 115, 142

summarize, 35, 59, 128

support, 35

survey, 4

visualize, 67, 200, 207

Drawing

Maps, 103

Grammar

Adverbial clauses, 96–97

Adverbs, 15

be, 75

Comparative adjectives, 45, 55, 63, 78

Conditional statements, 199

Contrary–to–fact conditionals, 199, 204

could and *might*, 172

Frequency adverbs, 15, 30

Future conditional statements, 121–122

Future time clauses, 19

Gerunds, 142, 143

Infinitives, 142

Information questions, 87–88

Modals, 172

must vs. *have to*, 49, 56

Past continuous, 75, 80

Past participles, 117

Possessive adjectives, 163

Possessive pronouns, 163

Prepositions, 143

Present perfect, 118

Requests, 175

Sequencing transitions, 51, 56

should, 196

Superlatives, 46, 55, 63

while, 75

Yes/No questions, 66–67

Group activities, 19, 57, 73, 81, 105, 133, 140, 157, 170, 173, 181, 197, 205

Listening

Attitudes at work, 162

Bill paying, 69

Communication at work, 176

Conversations, 70, 125

Goals, obstacles, and solutions, 18

Greetings, 5

Housing, 65

Job interviews, 150

Purchasing methods, 48

Study habits, 23

Time management, 26, 27

U.S. geography, 188

U.S. government, 194

Matching

Diseases, 116

Doctors, 115, 130

Employee benefits, 178

Health habits, 120

Job applications, 147

Job descriptions, 139

Problems and solutions, 196

Questions and answers, 87

Study habits, 25

U.S. geography, 188

Partner activities, 4, 5, 14–15, 20, 40, 45, 48, 62, 64, 67, 74, 76, 86, 88, 104, 115, 119, 126, 138, 140, 150, 152, 166, 176, 180

Pronunciation

Human body, 116

Information questions, 87

Making requests, 175

Pausing, 97

Word stress, 16

Reading

Abbreviations, 9

Advertisements, 41, 43, 54

Bill paying, 68

Charts, 19, 28, 39, 45, 46, 49, 66, 75, 87, 91, 118, 121, 142–143, 152, 163, 190, 199, 202

Classified Ads, 62, 78

Community issues, 195

Comparing information, 102

Conversations, 5, 117, 163

Daily activities, 95

Directions, 93–94

Educational goals, 9

Employee benefits, 169

Fitness information, 126, 128, 131

Goals, 17

Goals, obstacles, and solutions, 21

Help wanted ads, 144, 146, 155

Housing, 65

Illnesses and symptoms, 117

Information questions, 70

Job applications, 148

Job interviews, 150

Letters, 76

Lists, 86

Maps, 92, 94, 186

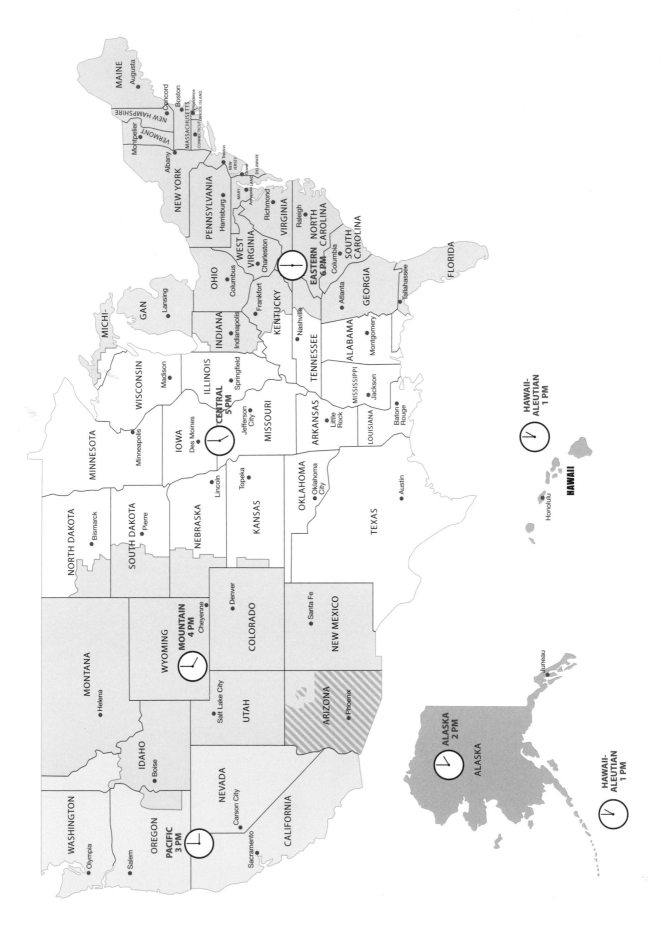